I dedicate this book to my husband, Brian, and mother, Clara. Your unconditional support, thoughtfulness, patience and love gave me the ability to create this book. I am one lucky girl to have you in my life!

I would like to acknowledge and thank all of the amazingly talented artists and Memory Makers staff who contributed to this book. Furthermore, I give thanks to my family and friends who continue to inspire and encourage me through my artful journey.

Erikia

table of *contents*

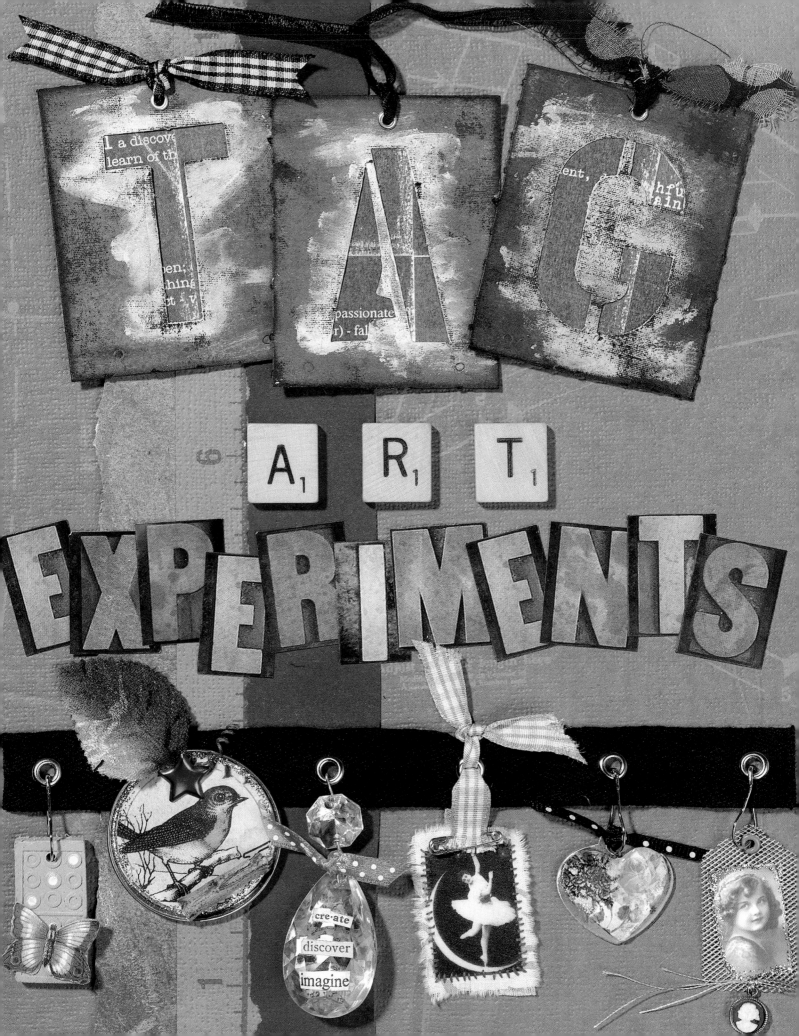

TAG

ART

EXPERIMENTS

Throughout my journey as a self-taught artist, I have discovered many lessons that have helped me grow into the artist I am today. One such lesson that has proven to be invaluable is the concept that experiments equal experience. As with most situations in life, we learn a great deal from our mistakes and achievements. This applies to the creation of art as well.

I spend a great deal of my time crafting engaged in experimentation. I love to try new techniques and work with materials in all-new ways to continuously push the boundaries of familiar products and mediums. Tags provide an ideal experimental canvas because they provide an absolutely perfect base with which to work. They can be of any shape, size, color, texture and material. Once adorned, tags can be used on numerous creations such as scrapbook pages, altered art, greeting cards, home décor crafts and much, much more.

Tags Reinvented showcases many of the distinctive materials and innovative techniques that I have stumbled upon while experimenting with tags, all of which are featured on my personal scrapbook pages throughout this book. To provide you with even more inspiration, I have collaborated with several very talented artists to compile nearly 200 additional tags based upon their interpretations of the materials featured. Furthermore, since this book encompasses a vast variety of materials and techniques, it has projects for scrapbook artists at every level.

I hope you enjoy this book and are motivated to refresh, renew and re-invent your approach to tag art based upon the unique creations you'll discover in the pages to follow. Moreover, that your artful journey of experimenting will bring you the experience and knowledge that you sought in this book!

Erikia

Erikia Ghumm
Author and Artist

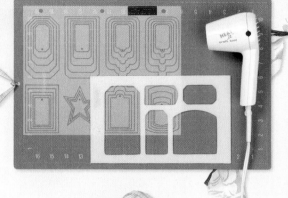

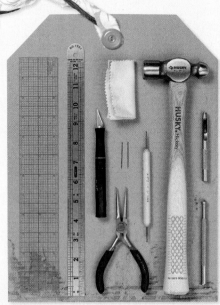

Tools

Stapler
Scissors
Craft knife
Burnishing and folding tool
Wood stylus
Needle-nose pliers
Eyelet setter
Hole punch
Hammer
Metal ruler
Plastic grid ruler
Circle punch
Tag templates
Lint-free sponge or cloth
Cutting mat
Needles

Adhesives

Tab applicator
Tape runner
Silicone adhesive
Liquid adhesive
Dot adhesive
Glue pen
Tape adhesive
Sheet adhesive

Colorants

Colored pencils
Paint pen
Acrylic paint
Fine-tip pen
Dual-tipped marker
Metallic rub-ons
Walnut ink

The tools pictured here are some of the basic tools needed for the creation of tag art. They are used in many of the projects featured throughout this book and would be beneficial to have on hand. Most of these tools are easily found in craft, hobby and hardware stores, if they are not already part of your scrapbooking toolbox. As you experiment with tags, you may find there are other tools you frequently use that should be added to your supplies arsenal.

Stamping Colorants

Pigment inkpad
Dye inkpad
Embossing inkpad
Solvent inkpad
Extra thick embossing powder
Embossing powder

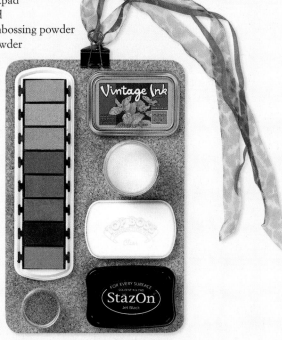

Machines

Adhesive application
machine
Die-cut machine
Label-making machine

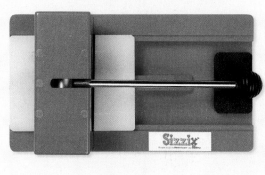

Stamps

Wood-mounted stamps
Unmounted stamps
Mounting blocks for
unmounted stamps
Homemade stamps
Rolling stamps

Applicators

Stipple brush
Foam-tipped stylus
Paintbrushes

Chemicals

Stamp cleaner
Photo cleansing solution
De-acidification spray
UV inhibitor
Solvent stamp cleaner

In addition to the aforementioned tools, there are several materials necessary for the creation of the tag art featured throughout this book. Because art is a personal expression and can be created in various styles by employing various methods, you may find that you wish to add your own favorite materials to this list as your work evolves.

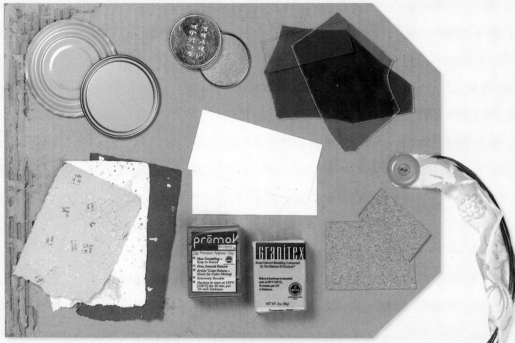

Materials for Creating Tags

Polymer clay
Glass
Handmade paper
Mica
Canvas

Manufactured Tags

Shipping
Circle metal-rimmed
Shaped metal-rimmed
Die-cut
Wooden
Plastic
Chipboard

Tag Toppers

Ribbons
Fibers
Clips
Fabrics
Twill
Velvet leaves
Plastic and soda tabs
Tassels and trim
Ball chain
Hemp
Twist ties
Paper cording

Decorative Accents

Ephemera
Beads
Game pieces
Charms
Postage stamps
Photo corners
Bottle caps
Photographic film
Glitter glue
Metal embellishments
Rhinestones
Hole reinforcements

Fasteners

Eyelets
Snaps
Brads
Staples
Paper clips
Thread
Nailheads
Safety and straight pins
Artist's tape
Buttons
Wire

TAGS *reinvented* 11

album tags

Using albums as a tag material or conversely, turning other materials into tag albums, offers several unique options for creating memory crafts. They can be cut to into different tag shapes and used in a multitude of ways depending on the materials and size of the album. Larger tag albums can function just like regular scrapbooks and smaller tag albums may be incorporated into scrapbook pages to contain journaling, additional photos, or may even be worn as jewelry. The easiest type of album to cut into a tag shape is one made from paper, but don't stop there; you can generate amazing results when using albums made from chipboard, old books and other scrapbook materials bound into a book and cut into a tag shape.

Materials list: *Paper album, craft knife, cutting mat, metal edged ruler, graduated circle punches, cardstock, ribbon and ink pad*

By simply cutting off two corner edges of this 5 x 7" paper album, it is transformed into a one-of-a-kind scrapbook. The cover has been adorned with the stamped words "Beauty Queen" by using unmounted alphabet stamps and clear acrylic blocks, which makes centering the words a cinch. Complete the look with rhinestones, frilly ribbons, inked pages, vintage cosmetics labels, colored bobby pins and glitter to create a glamorous scrapbook to treasure.

Soul Mates A super-mini scrapbook is transformed into a tag and adorned with a fabric flower and rhinestone from a vintage brooch. **"Younique Women"** Premade shipping tags are bound into an album with binding discs and a handcut plastic cover. **It's Random** A spiral-bound tag album is customized with stamps, rub-ons, ribbon and other unique materials. **Beauty, Mother, Create** A trio of collaged tags becomes a mini triptych album when attached with jump rings. **Born on the 4th of July** Collaged mini file folders sewn together and topped off with twill tape make an interesting tag album.

1 Using a craft knife and metal-edged ruler, trim off one corner of the album by slowly cutting through the layers with several cuts. Don't cut through the album too quickly because this will produce an uneven edge, which is hard to correct.

2 Add color to the plain pages in the album using an ink pad. Press it directly onto the pages in a random pattern until they are covered. Depending on the type of ink used and the pressure applied, the end result will vary. It may be a good idea to practice on scratch paper first to determine the desired effect.

3 Punch holes along the center outside edge of the album pages. Punch out hole reinforcements from cardstock by punching the smallest hole first, then re-punch.

Born on the 4th of July, *Cherie Ward*

Soul Mates, *Erikia Ghumm*

It's Random, *Marah Johnson*

Beauty, Mother, Create, *Marah Johnson*

Younique Women, *Erikia Ghumm*

alphabet stencil tags

Alphabet stencils are generally used with paint to label shipping crates, boxes and other industrial items. They are primarily constructed from paper, but also come in metal varieties. Typically, alphabet stencils are square or rectangle in shape and utilize a similar font style, giving them a widely recognizable look. However, now that alphabet stencils are used among scrapbookers, manufacturers are producing them in a wider variety of styles perfect for various artistic techniques. Look to the altered arts for ingenious ideas for stenciling bold words onto a background, decorating actual stencils as design elements, or turning stencils into tags.

Materials list: *Paper alphabet stencils, faux rust paint kit or brown, red and yellow liquid acrylic paint, fine sand, a sponge, spray bottle and piece of scratch paper*

Photos: *Brian Ghumm*

Here paper alphabet stencils are transformed into tags and use two different types of faux rust finishes to add to the roughness of this powerful scrapbook spread. Actual paper stencils are used for "Life" while the date tags "01-11-01" were created by using the stencils on torn cardstock strips. Combined with faux rust-textured stickers and walnut ink-stained papers, the extreme feelings of a life-altering event were dramatically represented.

Smile, *Erikia Ghumm*

Dad, *Nick Nyffeler*

Smile A printed alphabet stencil layered with painted cardstock is easily turned into a tag with a decorative paper clip and ribbon. **Howdy** The appearance of alphabet stencils is changed by wrapping them with fibers such as jute. **Fun With Letters** A Vintage alphabet stencil forms a tag base and is collaged with paper stencil letters, colorized mini metal stencils and printed paper. **Japanese K** A personal touch and added dimension is created using alphabet stencils with various stamped images and foam adhesive. **Dad** A masculine tag using leather paper and various metal accents is boldly titled with metal circle alphabet stencils.

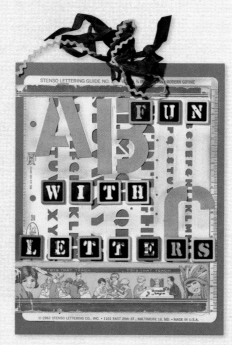

Fun With Letters, *Sarah Fishburn*

Howdy, *Jodi Amidei*

1 Working over a protected work surface, apply a coat of brown paint to an alphabet stencil using a sponge. While the paint is still wet, pour a small amount of sand onto the stencil. Apply another coat of paint, mixing in the sand. Allow to dry completely.

2 Using a water-moistened sponge, pick up a small amount of yellow paint. Daub it randomly over the stencil, blending it in slightly. This application should look uneven.

3 Blend a small amount of reddish-colored paint with water in a spray bottle, mixing thoroughly. Spray this mixture over the stencil, blending any runs with a moistened sponge. Repeat this application with brown paint.

Japanese K, *Kari Hansen-Daffin*

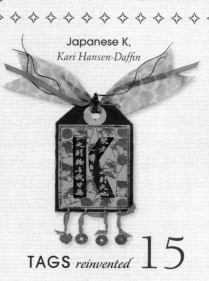

beaded tags

For thousands of years, beads have been assembled into jewelry or added to various objects for a decorative touch. They come in a plethora of varieties, colors, shapes and sizes, making the possibilities for embellishing endless. Small or flat beads are best to use on tags and other scrapbook adornments, as they do not indent photographs or other materials on a facing page when the album is closed. Beads can be applied to numerous materials using strong sheet adhesive, dimensional glaze, liquid glue and sewing, all of which depend on the type of material being utilized. For the best results, experiment with different adhesives before creating an entire project.

Photos: *Brian Ghumm*

Add flair, texture and dimension to a colorful layout by adding a mixed seed and bugle bead tag. Tie the spread together by incorporating the beads on another embellishment such as the photo corners featured on the opposing page of the layout. The secret to making the beads work on the tag is to use a cardstock base that matches the color of the beads and to add a smaller material such as glitter or micro beads to fill any gaps.

Materials list: *Cardstock, double-sided sheet adhesive, seed bead mix, loose glitter, alphabet beads, photograph, decorative eyelet, ribbon, tag die-cut machine or tag template and scissors*

Imagination, *Erikia Ghumm*

Merry Christmas, *Janetta Wieneke*

Life Is a Gamble Strung seed beads and liquid glue form a delicate frame sealed with gel medium. **Memories** Clear micro beads adhered with solid sheet adhesive on a preprinted tag create a diffused appearance. **Imagination** A liquid "paint on" bead mixture is applied to a chipboard tag along with sparkling glitter. **Four Girls and Their Horse** Dimension is easily added to a tag by sewing on beads in a contrasting color. **Merry Christmas** Beads pre-strung onto wire and wrapped around a tag add unique texture.

Life Is a Gamble,
Erikia Ghumm

Four Girls and Their Horse,
Sarah Fishburn

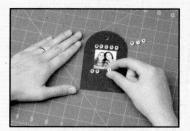

1 Apply strong double sided sheet adhesive to a cardstock base, leaving on the protective covering over the adhesive which is not adhered to the cardstock. Cut into a tag shape using a die-cut machine. Peel off the protective covering to expose the adhesive. Add photograph and alphabet beads to tag.

2 Place the tag into a small tray. Pour seed and bugle bead mix over the tag until covered. Press the beads firmly into the tag, making sure all are lying flat in a single layer and not hanging over the edges of the tag. Once finished, remove the bead mix from the tray.

3 Place the beaded tag into the bottom of the small tray again. Pour loose glitter over the tag, pressing it into the crevices between the beads. Firmly tap off any excess glitter. If any remains, uses a stiff brush to remove it from the surface.

Memories, *Erikia Ghumm*

bottle cap tags

In days gone by, soda pop was sold in glass bottles sealed with colorful metal bottle caps. Today, such things are novelties, making bottle caps an endearingly nostalgic tag material. Bottle caps come in a myriad of colors and designs ranging from vintage to modern. They can be purchased at flea markets; garage sales; antique, craft and scrapbook stores or from Internet companies and auction sites. A very practical means of amassing a bottle cap collection is to look on the ground in parking lots and streets. Most of the time, they are covered with a beautiful patina of rust, giving them a completely different look. Bottle caps can be used in countless ways as a tag material. Try flattening them, using them as tag toppers, or in their original form for distinctive adornments.

Materials list: *Vintage and new bottle caps, coated pliers or regular pliers, an old rag, anywhere hole punch, hammer and a sturdy work surface*

The bright and cheerful colors of vintage and new bottle cap tags add the perfect touch to this adorable toddler layout. This color scheme is played out with the use of decorative ball chains, hand-painted papers and ransom-style letter stickers, all juxtaposed with a distressed printed transparency and papers.

Photo: *Mary Anne Denney*

Adore Siblings Album, *Erikia Ghumm*

Ann Hall 1936, *Erikia Ghumm*

Fun at the Amusement Park, *Tricia Rubens*

God Bless America, *Jennifer Bertsch*

1 Flatten bottle cap using a pair of coated pliers or regular pliers, using an old rag to cover its "teeth." Start along the outside edge and work toward the center. Note: Vintage bottle caps may have a layer of cork on the underside. Remove cork and other materials from the underside before flattening.

2 Punch a hole for hanging near the edge of the bottle cap using an anywhere hole punch and hammer. Work on a solid, sturdy surface, as it will take several blows to the punch to get through the rigid metal.

3 Flip the bottle cap over and flatten out the newly punched hole along with any other areas that may need to be evened.

Bathing Beauty, *Erikia Ghumm*

Bathing Beauty Interest is added to a flattened bottle cap with a vintage reproduction image, glitter glue and chandelier crystal topper. **Adore Siblings Album** Specialty printed bottle cap embellishments add a whimsical touch to a handmade album. **Ann Hall 1936** A found, distressed bottle cap is transformed into a unique flower by adding a punched mesh flower, brad and soft velvet leaves. **God Bless America** Printed bottle caps are turned into a larger image when grouped together. **Fun at the Amusement Park** Flattened bottle caps are wired together and layered over a handmade printed paper tag.

can lid tags

The metal lids that seal cans of juice, biscuits, or jars of food are unexpectedly useful materials for scrapbook tags. They can be used as shallow shadow boxes for mini dimensional objects and are perfect for using on album covers and 3-D assemblages. These benefits, in combination with being particularly sturdy and moreover "free," make can lids great materials for tags. Try working with this highly versatile material to create outstanding tag embellishments that add a little personal flair to exceptional scrapbook projects.

Materials list: *Can lids, watch faces, watch parts, clear-drying dimensional glue, anywhere hole punch, hammer, ribbon, velvet leaves and ripped fabric*

Can lids from juice and biscuit containers seem unlikely materials to use when creating a soft, feminine layout. However, they add just the right touch when combined with other metal and faux metal elements such as watch parts, a spiral paper clip, chicken wire printed paper and sparkling glitter glue. These elements are juxtaposed with soft velvet leaves, silk ribbon, ripped fabric and off-white acrylic paint to create a truly shabby chic layout.

Photo Box 2003-2004 A decorative image stamped with solvent ink onto a mini biscuit tube can lid makes a superb photo box label. **Delight** The rusted patina of a found can lid has an earthy and rustic appearance unlike typical can lids. **Sheri and Mother** Printed can lids used for home canning make charming shabby chic tags when distressed with acrylic paint. **USA** A trio of graduated sizes of adorned can lids are wired together for a sentimental wall hanging. **The Length of Life** The appearance of a can lid is changed by cutting the center out and replacing it with metal mesh.

1 Working over a solid work surface, punch a hole near the edge of the can lid with an anywhere hole punch and hammer. Because the can lid is so sturdy, it may take more than one blow to the punch to create the hole.

2 Arrange watch face and parts around the outside edge of the can lid, leaving room for a photograph in the center.

3 Adhere the watch parts to the can lid by pouring a small amount of clear-drying dimensional glaze underneath the watch face and on top of the watch parts. Once the glaze is dry, adorn the tag with fabric accents.

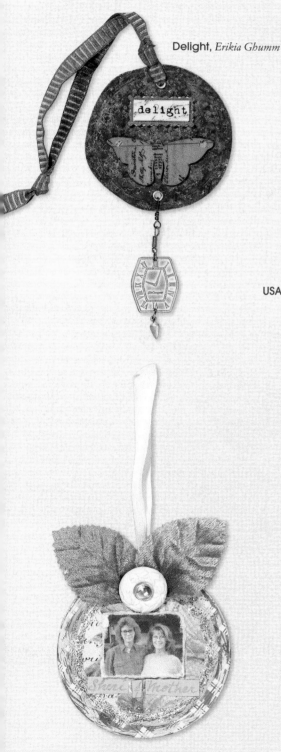

Delight, *Erikia Ghumm*

USA, *Holle Wiktorek*

Sheri and Mother, *Erikia Ghumm*

The Length of Life, *Kelly Angard*

Photo Box 2003-2004, *Erikia Ghumm*

canvas tags

Canvas is a sturdy, textured fabric used for innumerable items throughout the world. It is manufactured for use as a fabric, as backing for paintings, or as a type of computer printer paper. The fabric variety is usually a heavier bodied material used in everything from clothes to boat sails. Canvas manufactured for use as backing for paintings and as computer printer paper have a special coating, allowing paints and inks to adhere to their surfaces. Tags made from canvas exude many different themes depending on the form being used and the technique being applied. Try making everything from mini works of painterly art on printer-friendly canvas to rugged outdoorsy tags with hand-sewn canvas fabric.

Create retro-style tags easily by printing computer-generated images in black-and-white onto inkjet canvas and tinting them with oil photo-tinting paints. The sheet music represented on the tags was scanned and is hidden in the mini file folder decorated with the title "Souvenir Songs."

Materials list: *Inkjet canvas, digital images or computer clipart, oil photo tinting paints, waxed paper, cotton applicators (cotton balls and cotton swabs), artist's tape and paper trimmer, ruler, craft knife and cutting mat*

Happiness Painterly photographs are created by simply printing them onto inkjet compatible canvas. **Sweet Flowers** Textural canvas provides a perfect material for image transfers using copied images and gel medium. **Create your Dreams** Premade canvas tags are easily adorned with stamps and rub-on words. **Delight** A canvas tag is painted with acrylic paint in an artistic pattern along with a faux hole reinforcement. **Travel, Journey, Adventure** Using colored canvas for a tag background gives the material a completely different appearance.

1 Print black-and-white digital images or computer clip art onto inkjet canvas following the package directions. Cut out images, leaving a border around each with extra space at the top for adorning. Set up work area with waxed paper, oil paints and cotton applicators. Mask off edges and other chosen areas of the images using artist's tape.

2 Apply a very small amount of oil paint with a cotton applicator. For covering a large area, use a cotton ball and for a small area use, a cotton swab. Apply to the image in a circular motion until the desired effect is achieved. Remove the artist's tape. Allow images to dry several days before adorning and adding to a scrapbook page.

Happiness, *Erikia Ghumm*

Sweet Flowers, *Erikia Ghumm*

Delight, *Holle Wiktorek*

Travel, Journey, Adventure, *Tricia Rubens*

Create your Dreams, *Erikia Ghumm*

cardstock tags

From the beginning, cardstock has played a crucial role in scrapbooking. The most basic of supplies, it is available in an unimaginable spectrum of colors and textures, rendering it perhaps the most versatile material of the craft. The original cardstock tag is the basic shipping tag. Its characteristic shape has set the standard for most of the tags used in scrapbooking and other modern paper crafts. Not only do cardstock tags come in the classic shipping tag shape, they also come in a vast variety of other styles. Whether simple or elaborate, the widespread appeal of cardstock tags lies in their accessibility to scrapbookers of all styles and skill levels.

Create a faux mosaic tag by simply using scraps of cardstock for "tiles" and embossing powder for "grout." This unique, complex-looking technique is actually quite simple and is a perfect match for this graphic Asian-inspired layout. To make this superb tag stand out, it is layered on top of a light-hued paper along with a few other interesting embellishments.

Materials list: *Scrap cardstock, Xyron or solid sheet adhesive, circle cutter, rubber stamps, stamping ink, embossing powder, scissors, craft tray or scratch paper, burnishing and heat tool*

B and E, *Erikia Ghumm*

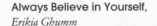

Always Believe in Yourself,
Erikia Ghumm

Fortune Cookie Flag Book, *Terri Zwicker*

1 Gather several pieces of scrap cardstock and stamp randomly over them. Cut the stamped cardstock into random straight edged "tiles" and set aside. Next, apply a solid adhesive to a larger cardstock piece. Cut it into a circle using a circle cutter. Apply the "tiles" to the adhesive-backed circle leaving at least ⅛" in between them.

2 Firmly burnish the "tiles" down to ensure they are adhered to the circle tag base. Flip the tag over and trim any excess with a pair of scissors.

3 Working over a craft tray or scrap paper, sprinkle contrasting-colored embossing powder on top of the tag. Tap off any remaining excess. Heat the embossing powder to melt it, which will take a bit longer to do than normal heat embossing of a stamped image.

B and E Plain cardstock is personalized through distressing with acrylic paint using a dry brush technique. **Always Believe in Yourself** Scraps of color-ized and stamped cardstock, printed papers and glitter form a faux mosaic. **Sing, Dance, Delight** Handmade cardstock tags with epoxy sticker embellishments are easily turned into custom-made party decorations with the addition of wooden skewers. **Tree Top, Chinese Silk, Patti Jo** Cardstock scraps are transformed into a mini paint chip sample. **Fortune Cookie Flag Book** Heavyweight cardstock is hand bound for a mini flag book.

Sing, Dance, Delight, *Clara Fricke*

Tree Top, Chinese Silk,
Patti Jo, *Sarah Fishburn*

TAGS *reinvented* 25

circle metal-rimmed tags

A typical business supply, circle metal-rimmed tags have been used for many years to identify items around the office. Their use in scrapbooking is similar, but certainly not limited to their original purpose. They are usually basic white, but also come in various colors and sizes. The blank surfaces of metal-rimmed tags just scream to be adorned with color, words, photographs and more using an array of techniques. The possibilities are unlimited, as these tags work well with other memory craft projects and 3-D assemblages.

Materials list: *Circle metal-rimmed tags, rub-on circles and alphabets, brads, craft markers, date stamp, waterproof dye ink and embossing stylus*

The whimsical, colorful tags on this spread were once white and completely unadorned. By layering the tag centers with rub-on transfers and letters in various fonts spelling "Hunter," they become vibrant. To finish the tags, they are adorned further with plain brads that are embellished with mini rub-on letters and a stamped date.

2 Create Album, *Erikia Ghumm*

Flower Seed Jar, *Erikia Ghumm*

Explosion of Laughter, *Clara Fricke*

Asian Invasion,
Torrey Miller

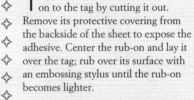

1 Apply an individual circle rub-on to the tag by cutting it out. Remove its protective covering from the backside of the sheet to expose the adhesive. Center the rub-on and lay it over the tag; rub over its surface with an embossing stylus until the rub-on becomes lighter.

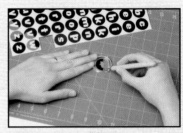

2 Apply the letters for the title to the tag on top of the colored backgrounds in the same manner as above.

3 Color in any areas that may have not been covered by the rub-ons or areas inside the letters with opaque craft markers. Stamp date using a waterproof dye ink and adhere the tags to the spread with brads that are decorated with mini rub-on letters.

ABC Book, *Sarah Fishburn*

2 Create Album A preprinted copper-rimmed tag is a quick and easy accent to add to a hand colorized circle tag album. **Flower Seed Jar** Individualized labels for storage are created with collaged circle-rimmed tags. **Explosion of Laughter** Circle-rimmed tags make excellent tag toppers when combined with ribbon. **ABC Book** A mini circle-rimmed tag book is easily created when bound with a loose-leaf paper ring. **Asian Invasion** The rim of a circle-rimmed tag is creatively colorized with embossing powder and are layered with smaller circle-rimmed tags using foam adhesive.

cd tags

Within the past few years, scrapbook artists have been looking to altered artists for inspiration. Thus the trend of altering objects for scrapbooks emerged, creating a whole new "look" within the craft. One material that has proven ideal for altering is the computer disc. With the digital age moving so quickly, components become outdated in a very short time, leaving behind useless software discs. Rather than throwing them out, these discs can be recycled and transformed into tags. They are ideal because they are inexpensive and often free, extremely flat and come furnished with a hole ideal for adding ribbon or other embellishments. Computer discs can be adorned with stamping, stickers, acrylic paints, alcohol inks and 3-D items.

Materials list: *Computer discs, various stamps, solvent stamping ink and cleaner, rub-ons and epoxy stickers*

Visually document the passage of time by using an old floppy disk and a modern CD as tags collaged with descriptive words from each respective time period. The sleek and graphic look of computer disk tags is mirrored in this layout with the use of vibrant techno-colored, graphic transparencies layered over printed paper.

Grab Happiness A mixed paper collaged tag is adorned with ribbon tied around a floppy disk and attached with staples. **Time Keeps on Passing** For added dimension a cut CD was stamped with images and dipped in extra thick embossing powder melted in a craft pot. **Silent Screen** Holes drilled through a collaged CD tag are strung with ribbon and beads for hanging. **Cool** Scraping off the reflective surface of a CD revealed the clear surface underneath which was then colorized with alcohol inks. **Boys Will Be Boys** A floppy disc boasts dimensional embellishments, distressed photographs and uniquely placed fibers.

1 Randomly stamp various text and image stamps over the computer disks using a solvent-based ink pad. The solvent-based ink pad is necessary for the images to be permanent on the slick plastic disks. If a mistake is made when stamping, simply remove it with solvent-based stamp cleaner.

2 Apply rub-ons randomly to the computer disks by removing its protective covering from the backside of the sheet, exposing the adhesive on the underside. Lay the rub-ons over the disc and rub over the desired words with an embossing stylus until they become lighter. Finish the disc with epoxy stickers.

Boys Will Be Boys,
Andrea Lyn Vetten-Marley

Grab Happiness, *Erikia Ghumm*

GRAB HAPPINESS
in the passing moments of life.

Silent Screen, *Jodi Amidei*

Cool, *Jodi Amidei*

Time Keeps on Passing,
Erikia Ghumm

cork tags

Cork is a natural material that has been present in crafting and decorating for several decades. Its smooth, resilient finish and earthy look makes it a choice material for several items such as the ever-popular memo board, coasters, lampshades, flooring, wall coverings and numerous crafts. The versatility of cork makes it an amazing material to work with when creating scrapbook tags because it can be punched, die-cut, painted, stamped, sewn, ripped, or burned with a hobby iron to create designs.

Photos: *Dennis Eriksen and Erikia Ghumm*

Step back into the 1970s when burning designs into wood and cork was popular home décor and apply it to your scrapbooks to create one-of-a-kind tags. The images featured on the tags are from an embroidery pattern, but other patterns such as rubber stamps, clip art and templates will also work.

Materials list: *A sheet of cork, iron-on patterns, household and hobby iron, ribbon, nailheads, craft knife, cutting mat and scissors*

Life's Little Lessons A decorative touch is added to a cutout in an album cover with a collaged square cork tag offset with sparkling glitter glue. **Artist's Motif No. 1** An artistic mosaic with stamped square cork stickers is layered over a plain red shipping tag. **Color and Texture** Printed cork letter stickers work well for words like "texture." **Yahoo** Dimensional laser-cut cork letters provide a fun and quirky title. **The Simple Life** Cork circle-rimmed tags are hung along the bottom of a country-themed tag to add additional space for embellishing.

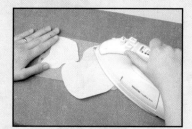

1 Cut cork into desired tag shape. Cut out iron-on patterns and apply them face-down onto the cork tag. Transfer them with a fabric iron set on high heat being careful not to move the patterns in the process.

2 Once the patterns are applied to the tag, burn the images and edges of the tag with a hobby iron that is fitted with a pointed tip. To achieve smooth flowing lines, let the iron heat fully before starting. Using very little pressure, draw the lines towards you, turning the tag as you move along to achieve a proper angle. Finish the tag with ribbon and nailheads.

The Simple Life, *Tricia Rubens*

Artist's Motif No. 1, *Erikia Ghumm*

Tip: Use caution when working with a hobby iron, as they become extremely hot and should never be left unattended or used by unsupervised children.

Color and Texture, *Marah Johnson*

Life's Little Lessons, *Erikia Ghumm*

Yahoo, *Tricia Rubens*

cyanotype tags

Cyanotypes, named after their alluring Prussian blue color, are a kind of chemically treated, light-sensitive photographic paper that reproduces images from black-and-white negatives, printed transparencies and various flat objects. The photographic process used to create the images on paper does not require a darkroom or extensive knowledge. Additionally, cyanotypes are archival, making them a superb material to incorporate into scrapbooks. Another beneficial quality of cyanotypes is that most of the pretreated papers are ideal for turning into tags because they can be cut very easily using scissors, a craft knife, punches or a die-cut machine.

The deep blue cyanotype tag featured on this page lends itself well to a tropical theme. The images on the tag are made from black-and-white photographic negatives, while found fabric pieces, a faux stamp, a compass, the stamped word "journey" and colored staples serve as embellishments. Group this strikingly beautiful tag with other vibrantly colored elements such as a title and oversized photograph to make a stunning statement.

Materials list: *Pretreated cyanotype paper, black-and-white negatives, a contact printing frame or a stiff board and piece of glass with smooth edges, rinsing tray, rubber gloves or tongs and paper towels*

Cherish Memories, *Andrea Lyn Vetten-Marley*

Tip: Use caution when working with cyanotypes as they are made from light-sensitive chemicals. As with any chemicals, precautions need to be taken. Never use tools that have been used for making prints for food preparation or storage and always use tongs or rubber gloves when handling wet prints.

1 Set up a work area with space to assemble the printing frame, a tray of water for rinsing the print and a place to allow it to dry. Begin by layering items in the following order: the printing frame or a stiff board, the pretreated cyanotype paper, black-and-white negatives and then the glass, making sure all the materials are in tight contact with one another. Expose the printing frame with layered materials to the sun according to the cyanotype paper package directions.

Family Heroes, *Erikia Ghumm*

Summer Field*

Summer Field, *Erikia Ghumm*

2 Once exposed, rinse the print in a tray of water for a few minutes, carefully agitating the print in the water until it no longer releases its cyan-colored chemicals. Remove it from the water and lightly blot dry with paper towels to absorb excess moisture. Set aside and allow to dry completely.

Photographs Album, *Erikia Ghumm*

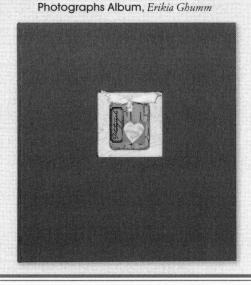

you hold the key to my

H E A R T

Key to my Heart, *Erikia Ghumm*

3 Cut into a tag shape by running the cyanotype print through a die-cut machine according to the manufacturer's instructions. Depending on the type of embellishments being applied to the tag, it may need to be adhered to a piece of cardstock before die cutting to add strength.

Summer Field A large format negative is printed onto cyanotype paper and die-cut into a tag shape. **Key to My Heart** Keys printed onto cyanotype paper make for an interesting tag background. **Family Heroes** A negative printed onto cyanotype paper results in an eye-catching photograph on a collaged tag. **Cherished Memories** Printed cyanotypes are adorned with stickers and rub-on words. **Photographs Album** A heart stamped onto a transparency acts as a negative for a cyanotype print.

TAGS *reinvented* **33**

die-cut tags

Die cuts were one of the first scrapbook embellishments when modern scrapbooking emerged in recent years. They are available in a plethora of themes, shapes, colors and styles. Turning them into tags not only gives them a fresh look, but is also a fantastic way to create uniquely personalized embellishments. They can be decorated with almost any medium or technique and altered to change or add to their appearance.

Materials list: *Die cuts, cardstock, graduated circle punches, alphabet stamps, waterproof dye ink, ribbon, foam adhesive, faux wax seal and scissors*

At first glance, the photographic sunflower die cuts on this spread seem an unlikely tag material, but when paired with stamped journaling, handmade hole reinforcements, ribbon and a faux wax seal, they create charming and whimsical tags just suited for the layout.

Wish You Were Here Die cuts are used figuratively to represent a vacation theme with a collaged suitcase. **Congratulations** Photographic die cuts are a fun alternative to the usual plain variety and make a quick adornment for tags. **Grandma** Graphic star-shaped die cuts are mated for a more sophisticated look. **Summer** Stamping inks and chalks provide a great solution for dressing up plain or lightly printed die cuts. **Girl Through Window** An intricately die-cut tag creates a unique look when layered with simple paper embellishments.

1 Punch a hole along the edge of the die cut. Punch out hole reinforcements from cardstock by punching the smallest hole first. Re-punch it by centering it inside a slightly larger hole punch. Add the reinforcement to the tag along with hand-dyed silk ribbon.

2 Stamp journaling using alphabet stamps and waterproof dye ink. If a mistake is made while stamping, immediately clean it off with a cotton swab soaked in waterproof dye ink cleaner. Adhere to the page using dimensional adhesive and embellish the largest die cut with a faux wax seal.

Wish You Were Here, *Erikia Ghumm*

Girl Through Window, *Sarah Fishburn*

Grandma, *Pamela Frye Hauer*

Summer, *Pamela Frye Hauer*

Congratulations, *Erikia Ghumm*

embossed paper tags

Embossed paper adds rich texture and dimension to any scrapbook layout. It can be purchased already embossed, or thin cardstock can be embossed by hand with paper crimpers or by using a light boxe with templates and a stylus. Even though purchased embossed papers come in several different patterns, styles and colors, hand embossing offers a particularly personalized touch. Embossed paper can be used as-is or may be colorized by wiping stamping ink pads directly across their surface, by applying chalk with a cotton ball, or by applying watercolor or pigment powders with a paintbrush and acrylic paints using a brayer. The creative potential of embossed paper is unlimited.

Materials list: *Cardstock shipping tags, paper crimper, light box, lettering template, stylus, and various colors of stamping ink-pads that have removable lids*

Personalize a special layout with a hand-embossed title and crimped shipping tags. The usual tone-on-tone effect of embossed paper, which can sometimes be hard to see, is accentuated on these tags with a quick and easy colorizing technique. The tags tie in nicely to the layout by boasting a monochromatic color scheme and incorporate such elements as words clipped from a vintage book, purple hand-painted paper and glitter glue highlights.

Amour Dark embossed paper is successfully colorized with opaque colorants such as light-colored stamping inks. **Lemonade** Larger embossed images painted with a wash of wet iridescent pigment powders create a stunning effect. **Got Style?** Specialty embossed papers give this tag a polished appearance. **Sweetness** Single color embossed papers lend subtle texture and a sense of elegance. **Focused** Embossed paper is made with the design applied to the surface, not in the paper.

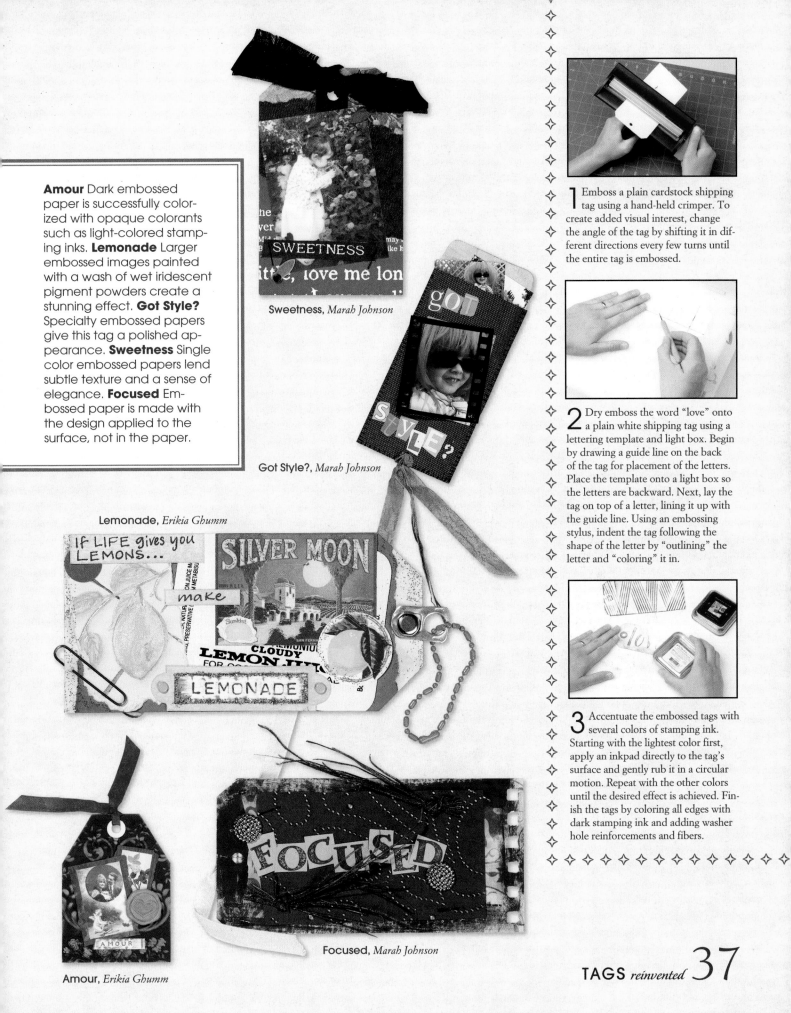

Sweetness, *Marah Johnson*

Got Style?, *Marah Johnson*

Lemonade, *Erikia Ghumm*

Amour, *Erikia Ghumm*

Focused, *Marah Johnson*

1 Emboss a plain cardstock shipping tag using a hand-held crimper. To create added visual interest, change the angle of the tag by shifting it in different directions every few turns until the entire tag is embossed.

2 Dry emboss the word "love" onto a plain white shipping tag using a lettering template and light box. Begin by drawing a guide line on the back of the tag for placement of the letters. Place the template onto a light box so the letters are backward. Next, lay the tag on top of a letter, lining it up with the guide line. Using an embossing stylus, indent the tag following the shape of the letter by "outlining" the letter and "coloring" it in.

3 Accentuate the embossed tags with several colors of stamping ink. Starting with the lightest color first, apply an inkpad directly to the tag's surface and gently rub it in a circular motion. Repeat with the other colors until the desired effect is achieved. Finish the tags by coloring all edges with dark stamping ink and adding washer hole reinforcements and fibers.

embossing foil tags

Embossing foil is thin, pliable metal sheeting that can be manipulated in a multitude of ways. It is traditionally available in silver, brass and copper, but also comes in a variety of bright colors closely resembling anodized aluminum. Its smooth, malleable surface can be engraved, embossed, lettered with steel stamps and colored with alcohol inks and paint. In addition, it may be shaped using scissors, a die-cut machine, punches and a plethora of other tools and techniques. Although embossing foil is supple, it is still a form of metal, which makes it great for decorating all types of scrapbook or memory craft projects where durability is essential.

Materials list: *Colored embossing foil, stylus, tag template, sanding block, hole punch, printed twist ties, and scissors*

Embossing foil tags make a perfect addition to this visually rough and worn page and have been manipulated to create a distinctive look cohesive with the rest of the elements. All the details are tied together by subdued colors, textured patterns and the incorporation of some embossing foil letters used in the mixed material names "Kirk and Heather."

Imagine, *Terri Zwicker (Inspired by Artist Tim Holtz)*

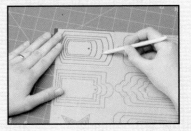

Kauai Sea Glass Jar, *Erikia Ghumm*

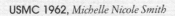

Be Yourself, *Kelly Angard*

USMC 1962, *Michelle Nicole Smith*

Girlfriends, *Holle Wiktorek*

1 Start by cutting a piece of colored embossing foil down to a manageable size. Next, handwrite a word into the surface of the foil using a stylus. If the impression of the word is not deep enough, it can be carefully retraced on a soft surface such as a mouse pad.

2 Working with a tag template, center the word inside the desired tag shape and trace the outline of the shape using a stylus.

3 Sand the surface of the foil in several directions to remove the color from the raised areas of the design. When the desired look is achieved, cut out the tag using an old pair of scissors and punch a hole at one end for the addition of a printed twist tie or other type of adornment.

Kauai Sea Glass Jar Embossing foil stamped with solvent ink is punched into a tag shape. **Imagine** Die-cut imagery is adhered to a shipping tag and covered with aluminum construction tape that has been colorized with alcohol inks and accentuated with black solvent ink. **Girlfriends** Embossing foil was cut into a whimsical flower shape. **USMC 1962** Steel letter stamps effortlessly create perfect recessed words in embossing foil tags. **Be Yourself** Heavy-gauge embossing foil is substantial enough to support several adornments and remains pliable for embossing.

epoxy sticker tags

Epoxy stickers are a relatively new product to the world of scrapbooking. Most epoxy stickers are clear, but they also come in several colors. In addition, they are available in numerous shapes and may be printed with a pattern, words or letters. Using epoxy stickers as tags presents a whole new look to a classic embellishment. They can be used as an entire tag base, as a decorative element, as a means to highlight areas of a design, or they may be layered with other materials to create a collaged look. Epoxy tags can be created to accommodate any scrapbooking style, allowing for a wide range of artistic interpretations.

Materials list: *Epoxy tag and regular letter stickers, words cut from book, gold leafing, stiff-bristled brush*

Transparent epoxy stickers make superb backdrops for layering other materials such as gold leafing. Combined with letter stickers and words cut from book pages, they create the tag title and journaling on this spectacular fall-themed layout. Golden tones carried through the design create a harmonious effect with the photographs.

Photos: *Brian and Erikia Ghumm*

Create Believe Imagine, *Erikia Ghumm*

Remember Family History, *Erikia Ghumm*

1 Adhere individual letter stickers to the underside of the epoxy sticker tags. Repeat with words cut from book pages.

2 Apply gold leafing to the sticky underside of the tags, pressing it into place. For convenience, store gold leafing in a shallow tub, which makes it easy to work with.

3 Brush off excess gold leafing using a stiff-bristled brush.

Create Believe Imagine A personalized tag background is created with printed epoxy stickers layered over cardstock colorized with stamping inks. **First Class Letters** A plain epoxy tag sticker is transformed into a mini collage with reproduction ephemera offset with sparkling glitter. **Remember Family History** Word-and-letter printed epoxy stickers set in stylish conchos are used to alter an old 45 record. **Hugs and Kisses** Clear epoxy stickers are perfect for highlighting slide mount frame elements placed over a photograph. **Hold Me Tight** Epoxy tag stickers are layered with printed transparencies and pressed flowers for a nostalgic feel.

First Class Letters,
Erikia Ghumm

Hugs and Kisses, *Marah Johnson*

Hold Me Tight,
Emily Curry Hitchingham

fabric tags

The fluidness and rich texture of fabric add a special handmade touch to any scrapbook layout. When turned into tags, fabric becomes an undeniably sumptuous embellishment. Available in countless colors, patterns, styles, textures and new and vintage varieties, fabric can be used as a tag base material or as an adornment. It may be ripped, painted, dyed, die cut or may be adorned with image transfers or stamping. Attaching fabric to tags is quite simple through the use of sewing, stapling, gluing, brads and eyelets. Not only does fabric make for beautiful tags, it is also an ideal material for tag toppers for a personal touch.

The sweet photographs of a great-grandmother are turned into shabby chic tags when transferred onto vintage fabrics. The different patterns of the fabric and vintage handkerchief and tablecloth are pertinent to the style. The look is continued to the background with torn and sanded floral paper and solid green cardstock treated with white stamping ink.

Materials list: *Plain vintage or new fabric scraps, inkjet iron transfer paper, digital or scanned photographs, scissors, household iron and ironing board, sewing machine or thread and needle*

Heritage Photographs Album Shabby chic style is created using vintage fabrics, a silk flower and a velvet leaf assembled on a walnut-inked tag. **Inspire Romance** Luxurious fabrics and tapestries form a truly elegant tag. **You Define Love** Various types of fabric are unified with colorants like walnut ink and other dyes for a personal touch. **Flower Girls** A small piece of scrap fabric is cut with decorative scissors to provide added interest. **Wish** Fabrics printed with imagery make for quick, easy and texture-rich adornments.

1 Print scanned or digital photographs in reverse onto inkjet iron transfer paper according to package directions. Cut out photographs from sheet, leaving a slight border around them. Tear plain fabric into small pieces slightly larger than the images. Place images facedown onto the torn fabric and heat set according to package instructions.

2 Sew the photographic cloth images onto a handmade fabric tag in a haphazard fashion. Adorn the top with silk ribbon attached with vintage straight pins.

Flower Girls, *Sarah Fishburn*

Inspire Romance,
Andrea Lyn Vetten-Marley

Heritage Photographs Album,
Erikia Ghumm

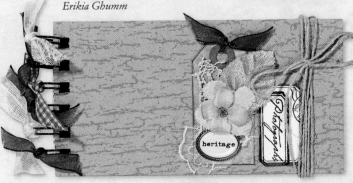

You Define Love,
Andrea Lyn Vetten-Marley

Wish, *Marah Johnson*

fusible fiber tags

Fusible fiber is a new material to scrapbooking and can be purchased in yardage, as sheets, or as unformed fibers in a myriad of colors, some with an opalescent finish. When unformed, fusible fibers may be heated with a household iron to melt the fibers together, or they may be formed by hand for other creative options not available with preformed sheets. Fusible fiber can be molded into different textures using rubber stamps or any other heat-resistant material. When formed into a solid material, fusible fibers may be easily cut into tag shapes using scissors, a craft knife, a die-cut machine or punched when layered with paper for added substance. Fusible fiber tags and embellishments can be attached to layouts with liquid glue, solid sheet adhesive, sewing, staples, paper clips, brads and eyelets.

A touch of magic is added to photos of a childhood trip to Disneyland with colorful, opalescent fusible fiber tags. The shimmering touch they add to this playful spread is continued with the use of sparkling glitter glue and epoxy stickers.

Photos: *Dennis Eriksen*

Materials list: *Unformed fusible fibers in different colors, craft fiber cut into "confetti" pieces, cardstock, Xyron or solid sheet adhesive, die-cut machine with tag die or punch, thin scratch paper, household iron and ironing board*

Halloween Greetings,
Erikia Ghumm

Asian Infusion,
Tricia Rubens

Miracle, *Andrea Lyn Vetten-Marley*

Live in My Heart, *Erikia Ghumm*

1 Mix several different colors of unformed fusible fibers by loosely forming them into a ball and pulling them apart. Repeat the process until the desired effect is achieved. Lay the mixed fibers onto a thin piece of scrap paper atop an ironing board.

2 Sprinkle some of the "confetti" cut fibers on top of the mixed fibers. Add a very thin layer of unformed fusible fibers (used to hold the cut fibers in place) and a thin piece of scratch paper. Melt the fibers together with a household iron following the package instructions.

3 Take the newly formed sheet and adhere it to a piece of cardstock that has a solid adhesive applied to it. Cut this layered piece into a tag shape with a die-cut machine or punch.

Hold Me,
Erikia Ghumm

Live in My Heart Fusible fibers are molded by layering them on a rubber stamp covered with thin paper and heat setting them with a household iron. **Halloween Greetings** Several colors of fusible fibers are combined into a thin layer for a wispy tag background. **Hold Me** Fusible fibers are shaped with a paper stencil, heat-set, colorized with stamping ink and heat-set again. **Asian Infusion** Combining fusible fibers with other textural handmade papers gives tags a tailored appearance. **Miracle** Fusible fibers are used like fabric and are sewn to a wire support hung from beads.

glass tags

With its sleek and smooth finish, glass has attracted artists of all types for centuries. Its use in scrapbooking is fairly recent and has been adapted from the altered arts. The most popular glass material in scrapbooks has been the microscope slide, which can be easily transformed into a tag. Other glass tag options come in the form of optometrist lenses, stained-glass pieces and formed pieces of glass. Glass tags may be decorated by stamping (use a solvent-based stamping ink), etching (cream or with an engraving tool) or coloring (use alcohol-based inks and craft markers). Additionally, try applying metal tapes, transparencies (use solid sheet adhesive), stickers or rub-ons.

Materials list: *Shaped glass tag, rub-on letters, embossing stylus, dimensional adhesive*

Mimic the beautiful look of sea glass with the use of teal and green decorative glass corners and a glass tag. The vintage photographs of the vacationing couple featured in this spread are layered against a printed collaged paper. Sanding and treating stamped, hand-colored seashells and reproduction photographs with white stamping inks blends them subtly into the background.

Remember, *Erikia Ghumm*

Love Album, *Erikia Ghumm*

1 Apply rub-on letters to the glass tag by removing the protective covering from the backside of the sheet to expose the adhesive on the underside. Lay the rub-ons over the tag and rub over the desired letters with an embossing stylus until they become lighter.

2 Drizzle or brush on a thin layer of clear-drying dimensional glaze, covering the entire tag surface. Allow to dry.

Le Pont de Salata Constantinople A vintage photographic slide is layered between glass pieces and the edges are sealed with copper tape and silver solder. **Remember** Printed transparencies are added to glass microscope slides with a layer of solid sheet adhesive. **The Roses Have Faded** Glass tags are adorned with dimensional embellishments adhered with strong bonding silicone glue. **Love Album** Words and imagery are easily etched into glass tags with a hobby engraving tool. **Dichroic Illusions** Faux dichroic glass is created with a simple application of transparent opalescent plastic sheeting adhered with a thin layer of dimensional glaze.

Dichroic Illusions, *Jodi Amidei*

Le Pont de Salata Constantinople,
Erikia Ghumm

The Roses Have Faded, *Erikia Ghumm*

handmade paper tags

Most handmade papers are richly textured and have an earthy appearance that is completely astounding. Available in a vast variety of textures, colors and styles, no two pieces are exactly alike. A dramatic departure from cardstock, handmade paper gives any scrapbook project a sense of simple sophistication and turns an ordinary embellishment into an extraordinary one. Handmade paper tags can be made using a paper-making kit or simply by using purchased handmade papers. The advantage to making paper at home is that it can make artful use of scraps and other toss-away items, such as bits of ribbon, fibers, confetti and dried plant material. Moreover, the expense of purchased handmade paper makes creating your own a beautiful and resourceful way to recycle. If using non-scrapbook materials to make paper, an additive can be used to make the paper acid-free.

Materials list: *A ready-made paper-making kit or a hand mold with screens, couch (drying) papers and sponge, blender, cookie sheet, vat (dishpan or storage container), turkey baster, tag deckle (template), a paper press, heavy books or iron for drying papers, cardstock torn into small pieces, inclusions of ground mica, copper leafing and red dried flowers*

A striking close-up photograph of a flower is set against a layered backdrop of magnificent handmade papers on this colorful layout. All the page needs for embellishment is one adorned handmade paper tag with a printed canvas photograph, velvet leaves and silk ribbon attached with a copper spiral paper clip. To adhere all of the papers to the cardstock base, a strong foam adhesive is used to ensure a permanent bond.

He Loves Me He Loves Me Not This handmade paper tag is given added interest with naturally distressed stamped imagery from the paper's roughly textured surface. **Nurture Life** Torn handmade papers are collaged and die cut into an artistically pieced tag. **Grandmother** A natural theme is emphasized by adding dried pressed flowers to a collaged handmade paper tag. **Life Is Good** Paper flowers add a playful touch to feminine handmade paper tags. **Stick Your Neck Out!** A cardstock tag is layered with torn pieces of handmade paper that hang over its edges.

1 Set up a work area with all of the tools and supplies listed. Fill the blender with a few cups of water, torn pieces of cardstock and various inclusions. Blend until the desired texture is achieved.

2 Set the hand mold in the vat with tag deckle inside. Add the pulpy paper mixture to the tag deckle using a turkey baster until the form is completely filled in.

3 Remove the tag deckle from the hand mold. Then, remove the bottom screens of the hand mold and place them onto the cookie sheet. Lay a cover screen over the surface of the newly formed tags and remove the moisture with the sponge. Absorb more of the water using the couch sheets. Once the water is removed, dry the tag(s) using an iron, or press between couch sheets using heavy books or a paper press.

Grandmother, *Tricia Rubens*

He Loves Me He Loves Me Not,
Erikia Ghumm

Stick Your Neck Out!, *Jennifer Pollman*

Nurture Life, *Erikia Ghumm*

Life Is Good, *Tricia Rubens*

mat board tags

Mat board is composed of several layers of compressed paper and is fairly similar to chipboard. The difference is that the compressed layers of mat board are usually white, have a special paper finish on the surface and are usually made with archival materials. The sturdiness of this material makes it ideal for applying wet mediums and using it for other types of memory crafts. The one thing to remember when working with mat board is that it is best cut using a craft knife and metal-edged ruler.

This mat board tag adds a grand presence to this graphic layout. Its dimension and thickness create a look that cannot be achieved by using any other materials. The thickness is further accentuated with black stamping ink, which covers the white compressed layers. A photograph, journaling and ribbon complete the tag for the layout.

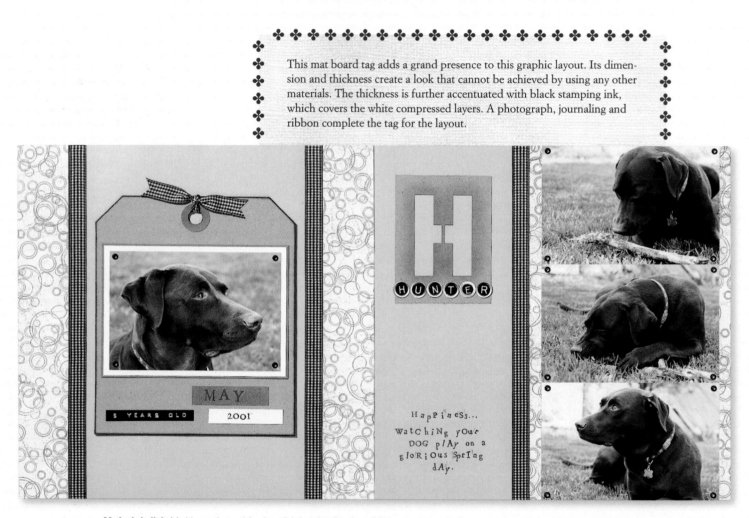

Materials list: *Mat board, cardstock, solid sheet adhesive, ribbon, stamping ink, hole punch and anywhere hole punch in graduated sizes, hammer, cutting mat, metal-edged ruler, craft knife*

Soul Paintings, *Erikia Ghumm*

Smile,
Erikia Ghumm

The Real West,
Erikia Ghumm

Crow, *Torrey Miller*

Child of Adoption Easel Frame,
Erikia Ghumm

1 Cut a piece of mat board into a manageable piece, just slightly larger than the desired tag. Cover with cardstock that has been backed with solid sheet adhesive. Draw tag shape onto the cardstock-covered mat board and cut out using a craft knife and metal-edged ruler. For perfect edges, make several cuts instead of one to cleanly get through the mat board.

2 Working over a solid work surface, punch a hole near the top center edge of the tag with an anywhere hole punch and hammer. Because the mat board is so thick, it may take more than one blow to the punch to create the hole.

3 Accentuate the dimension of the tag by inking its edges with stamping ink. Simply hold the tag at a 45-degree angle and wipe it across the surface of an inkpad, or hold the inkpad in one hand and the tag in the other and apply the ink to the edges by wiping the inkpad onto the tag.

The Real West Placing a mini collage behind circle openings in die-cut mat board provides structure and visual weight. **Smile** Crackle modeling paste applied to a mat board tag washed with walnut ink exudes texture. **Soul Paintings** Vintage paint-by-numbers on mat board makes for an off-the-wall tag. **Child of Adoption Easel Frame** A plain black die-cut mat board frame is transformed into a tag with an oversized decorative eyelet and silk ribbon. **Crow** Cardboard, an inexpensive alternative to mat board, is easily turned into a tag with paint and collage materials along with a hole cut in the top for adding fibers.

mesh tags

Since its introduction into the world of scrapbooking, mesh has proven to be a multipurpose material that can be incorporated into almost any scrapbooking style. It is suitable to use on everything from a layout background to a tag embellishment. Mesh is manufactured in a wide variety of forms such as metal, fiber and paper. Additionally, it is available in multiple textures, patterns and colors. Mesh can be used to create tags in several ways, including layering, die cutting, punching, ripping, colorizing and much more. For attaching mesh, experiment with stapling, sewing, gluing and attaching with brads or eyelets for possible options. Some varieties of mesh even come in self-adhesive forms.

Materials list: *Various colors and shades of self-adhesive roll mesh, decorative eyelets, hammer, cone eyelet setter, hole punch and scissors*

Brightly colored, layered mesh tags and photo corners add a distinctive touch to this lovely garden-themed spread. Layering the mesh adds visual weight and depth to the material without it losing its airy look. The mesh accents complement the whimsical photo of the pink sunflower, which has been manipulated using image-editing software. Other unique additions include faux wax seals, sparkling glitter glue, Dymo labels and words cut from old books.

Maddy, *Marah Johnson*

Crazy M, *Marah Johnson*

Girlfriend Album An album cover is embellished with punched copper mesh flowers adhered to a fabric-covered tag with rhinestone brads. **Crazy M** Metal mesh is applied to a collaged tag for texture and balance. **Kennedy** Fine metal mesh serves as an attachment when used with brads and eyelets. **Maddy** Printed transparencies are layered over soft mesh made from twine for contrast. **Copper Leaf** Mesh is framed within two oversized bookplates for an airy effect.

1 Working with two different shades of self-adhesive mesh, cut about 6" off each roll. Layer the two pieces of mesh together.

2 To create the top of the tag, simply fold the mesh in half and trim from the end point to the non-folded side to create a point.

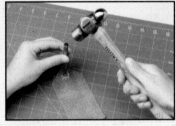

3 Punch a hole in the top center of the tag. Add a decorative eyelet to complete the look and for reinforcement of the hole. If using nonstandard eyelets, set them over a very sturdy work surface using a full-sized hammer.

Kennedy, *Marah Johnson*

Copper Leaf,
Emily Curry Hitchingham

Girlfriend Album,
Erikia Ghumm

mica t a g s

Mica is a natural transparent mineral that is formed in solid blocks consisting of countless layers. It is mined all over the world and is used in the electrical and crafting industries. Mica as a scrapbooking material emerged a few years ago as a crossover from rubber stamping. It can be purchased in solid sheets sometimes referred to as "tiles" or as ground granules or flakes. Solid sheet mica is generally the form used for scrapbooking. This acid-free material is easily cut into tag shapes using various cutting tools. Each cut piece then can be separated into several more pieces. It can be stamped, heat embossed, painted and adorned in countless other ways. Additionally, there are several ways to attach mica. Try using staples, sewing, paper clips, brads, eyelets and clear-drying liquid glue. With all of its uses, mica is a unique tag material and is also extremely economical.

Materials list: *A large sheet of mica, hole punch, craft knife, ruler and cutting mat*

The large handcut mica tags covering the pages of this unique spiral-bound album complement an outdoors theme. The mica is attached to the pages with large decorative eyelets, a paper clip and a metal label holder attached with mini brads. The photographs are set against a fiery acrylic paint background and the theme is rounded out with the addition of vintage fish collage paper, velvet leaves and fibers.

Art and Soul Mica is used as accent pieces on a mixed-media tag. **Spiritual** A simplistic tag is layered with mica to add interest without overwhelming the design. **Smile** Attention is drawn to photographs by layering them with mica. **Fifties Foods** A collage is sealed in between mica sheets with decorative metal tape. **Southwestern Tag** Both sides of mica are stamped, heat embossed and embellished with wire and beads.

1 Cut sheet mica into a tag shape using a craft knife and ruler. The mica is easily cut, but it will take several passes with the craft knife to get through all of its layers.

2 Make a mark at the center top of the tag for a hole. Punch out with a hand punch.

3 Using a craft knife, separate the layers by inserting the sharp point into the edge of the mica. Once started, the layers are easily separated by gently peeling them apart. Repeat as many times as desired.

Spiritual, *Marah Johnson*

Fifties Foods, *Cherie Ward*

Southwestern Tag, *Torrey Miller*

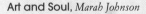

Art and Soul, *Marah Johnson*

Smile, *Marah Johnson*

modern ephemera t a g s

People are surrounded by modern ephemera every day. Consisting of everything from junk mail, receipts, tickets and other "useless" paper items, these tiny pieces of daily life can speak volumes about who we are and the times we live in. This makes modern ephemera an ideal material to transform into tags for scrapbooking. For a unique twist, look for not-so-obvious modern ephemera pieces, such as product packaging and labeling. Also, look for special finds on the ground in parking lots, streets and parks. The only drawback to using modern ephemera is that it usually is not archival. However, there are several modifications that can be made if such is a concern. Printing pieces onto archival paper using a scanner and printer or copy machine, sealing with laminate, or spraying items with a de-acidifying and UV inhibitor are potential solutions.

Photos: *Becca Payson & Erikia Ghumm*

Nothing could better document a successful day of shopping with a friend than using the price tags from purchased items as embellishments. With the simple addition of stapled ribbon and sparkling glitter glue, these commonplace items are magically transformed into unique tags. Other colorful additions such as vintage rickrack, shabby floral fabric and mismatched mosaic printed paper all round out the kitschy theme.

Materials list: *Modern ephemera, ribbon, staples, glitter glue*

He Drinks a Latte, *Erikia Ghumm*

Looking for a Car, *Clara Fricke*

Breakfast (6:00) at Tiffany's,
Sarah Fishburn

Lantern Party, *Sarah Fishburn*

Going Crazy, *Tricia Rubens*

He Drinks a Latte A paper cup is transformed into a tag by cutting out the bottom, flattening it and adhering it together with staples. **Looking for a Car** An image on a tag is exposed by cutting through several layers of newspapers layered on top of it. **Breakfast (6:00) at Tiffany's** Decorative product packaging forms a stylish tag base. **Lantern Party** An embossed business card holder is collaged with images and stickers. **Going Crazy** Collaged and stamped travel tickets and tags make a larger single tag.

negative tags

Negatives play a big part in scrapbooking, but only behind the scenes. It was not until recently that they actually made their debut as a scrapbook embellishment. Negatives come in several different types, such as undeveloped film, processed film and printed transparencies, all of which come in a plethora of shapes and sizes. They can also be made using stamps, die-cut machines and punches. Negatives are an unusual yet fitting material that works well for creating tags. Their uses are very similar to transparencies and make for excellent tag backgrounds and adornments. Another fantastic quality of negatives is that the actual film types are usually "free" because they are part of the photographic process.

Materials list: *Negatives from undeveloped film, processed film and printed transparencies, cardstock, alphabet stamps, dye stamping inks, decorative nailheads, mouse pad, wood craft stick, craft knife and cutting mat*

The various types of negatives used to create the title and photo mat tags on this artsy spread perfectly convey the photographic theme. A selective color palette drawn from the negatives creates design harmony, allowing the high-contrast black-and-white photographs of New York to stand out. Other distinctive elements that add to the spread are printed black artist's tape, distressed papers and a distorted negative contact sheet.

Discover Nature A negative-printed transparency is collaged with die cuts and stickers and is topped off with an undeveloped film tab. **Cherish, Faith, Inspire** Negatives are cut into small angled tags in graduated sizes and are adorned with textural fibers and stickers. **You Are My Sunshine** A negative strip is embellished with mini circle-punched photographs, paper and stickers. **Where There Is Love** Words and images are stamped onto negative strips using acrylic paint. **Pretty in Pink** Negative strips are framed with specialty papers and fabrics and are held together with a sewn zigzag stitch over a paper background.

1 Create the title for the page by stamping individual letters onto cardstock and cut or tear them out.

2 To give the stamped letters a distressed look, simply lay them face down, one at a time, onto the surface of a dye stamping ink pad. With very little pressure, rub over its surface to transfer the ink.

3 Adhere the stamped letters to the negatives and add a decorative nailhead topper.

You Are My Sunshine, *Pamela Frye Hauer*

Pretty in Pink, *Cherie Ward*

Cherish, Faith, Inspire,
Pamela Frye Hauer

Where There Is Love,
Holle Wiktorek

Discover Nature, *Erikia Ghumm*

page protector t a g s

Page protectors are an essential component of most types of scrapbooks and exist to protect precious photographs and layouts from damage. Page protectors are typically made from high-quality archival plastic and come in innumerable sizes and formats. A seemingly atypical material for creating scrapbook tags, page protectors have certain qualities unmatched by any other material. They are quite resilient and can withstand many techniques. Fun things to try include coloring page protectors with inks formulated to dry on nonporous surfaces, painting, stamping and applying rub-ons. In addition, they can be turned into pocket tags by sewing or by sealing them with a hobby iron, making it possible to safely incorporate items onto a scrapbook page you otherwise could not.

Documenting a cat's life becomes visually interesting when materials such as cat food, catnip and a cat toy are added to a layout. Safely sealed in page protector pocket tags, these unusual materials give this retro-style spread a tangible quality like nothing else could. To emphasize the cat theme and to tie the spread together, sheer leopard print ribbon is added to the background and the quirky tags.

Materials list: *Page protectors, hobby iron with pointed tip, metal ruler, a thick pad of paper to use as a work surface, tag drawn onto paper to use as a template and objects or materials to put into the tags*

FLORIDA SUNRISE

Florida Sunrise, *Erikia Ghumm*

ART SPIRIT inspire

Art, Spirit, Inspire, *Erikia Ghumm*

Birthday Greetings

Birthday Greetings, *Erikia Ghumm*

Keep your face to the
sunshine
and you cannot see the shadows.
-Helen Keller

Keep Your Face to the Sunshine, *Janetta Wieneke*

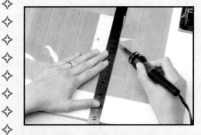

1 Place cardstock tag template on top of a thick pad of paper. Layer with two pieces of a page protector. Working with a hobby iron and metal ruler, "cut" out the tag, which will seal the edges at the same time. Leave one side uncut.

2 Open up the uncut/unsealed side of the page protector pocket. Add a material or object, leaving it to be sealed without puckering.

3 Seal the remaining edge by "cutting" it with the hobby iron and metal ruler. If desired, the hole for the top of the tag can also be cut/sealed by simply pushing the tip through at a 90 degree angle.

Thank You Card, *Erikia Ghumm*

THANKS

for the flowers!

Florida Sunrise A page protector is transformed into a tag wall hanging by cutting a slit in the back, sealing the top loading edge and adding eyelets for hanging. **Thank You Card** Dried flower petals are preserved in a page protector tag using a circle-rimmed tag for a base. **Birthday Greetings** A shaker tag is created by sewing a "pocket" onto a page protector and filling it with confetti. **Art, Spirit, Inspire** Alcohol inks and rub-on words colorize a page protector tag. **Keep Your Face to the Sunshine** Stamped images and dimensional adornments provide artful enhancements.

paper photo frame t a g s

In days gone by, studio portraits were displayed in decorative paper photo frames. These frames came in an assortment of styles from plain to elaborate. Typically they were of a neutral color and were printed with patterns, had an embossed design, or both. Most frames are vintage, but now select companies are offering reproductions. The vintage variety can be purchased from garage sales, antique stores, Internet shops and auction sites for a few dollars apiece. Moreover, friends and relatives may also have vintage frames stowed away in their attics that they would be willing to pass on. Paper photo frames may seem like an uninteresting material to turn into tags, but when adorned with a tag topper, they are completely transformed into one-of-a kind embellishments.

This colorful shabby chic spread features a large vintage paper photo frame decorated with various text images. The frame is turned into a tag with the addition of a paper tab and decorative eyelet. The smaller frames are reproductions and are aged so that they coordinate with the style of the spread. For a touch a femininity, sparkling glitter glue has been used to highlight the frame tags. Vintage bark cloth floral paper, chartreuse silk ribbon and a vintage belt buckle complete the look.

Materials list: *Vintage and reproduction paper photo frames, decorative stencil, various stamps and dye stamping inks, foam-tipped blending tool*

A Rose-Colored World, *Erikia Ghumm*

Altered Photo Frame, *Jodi Amidei*

Treasure A paper photo frame is personalized with stamped images and given dimension with foam adhesive. **A Rose-Colored World** The designs on a printed paper frame are highlighted with different colors of glitter glue. **Altered Photo Frame** A paper frame is altered with printed papers, decorative tape and dimensional glaze. **Sierra and Gina** A die-cut window tag with cellophane is used to frame a photograph and hold confetti. **My Heart Flutters** A photo frame provides a base for a decorative collage tag.

1 Stamp various text stamps using a dark-colored dye ink over a vintage paper photo frame, covering it completely.

2 Place a text stencil over the stamped frame. Holding it down securely, color in the open areas of text with a lighter shade of ink and a foam-tipped blending tool. For best results, work the ink into the stencil using a circular motion.

3 To re-create the aged look on the smaller reproduction paper frames, colorize them with tan-colored dye inks. Finish the tags with paper tabs secured with eyelets.

Sierra and Gina, *Sarah Fishburn*

My Heart Flutters,
Pamela Frye Hauer

Treasure, *Erikia Ghumm*

pet identification tags

Pet identification tags are widely used by pet owners to aid in the return of their beloved companions should they become lost. Their smooth, thin and lightweight metal makes them an ideal material for scrapbooking. They also come in plastic, but the metal form is considerably thinner and easier to obtain. They can be purchased at pet supply stores and super centers that have a special engraving machine on their premises. These engraving machines are easy to use and only take a few minutes. The fantastic thing about these tags is that you can have almost any word or words perfectly engraved into a multitude of tag shapes and colors.

Materials list: *Engraved pet identification tag, ribbon, decorative nailhead, foam spacer, scissors*

An American soldier is not complete without symbolic, honorary badges and medals. Honor these special individuals with a homemade badge that contains personal sentiments or aspects of his or her personality and involvement in the service. On this page, to create a more lifelike effect, the black-and-white photograph is enlarged so that the pet identification tag is more to scale. A small length of ribbon, which is folded over at the top, is attached to the tag and anchored with a small star nailhead and foam adhesive.

Heritage Photo Box Pet identification tags are personalized with steel letter stamps and accentuated with metallic rub-ons. **Travel Album** Images and words are stamped onto pet identification tags with solvent stamping ink and added to a hand-bound album. **Her Tender Heart** Rub-on words and decorative graphics embellish a pet identification tag. **Adore** Pet-themed tags are accented with identification tags. **Dog Tags** Circle pet identification tags are layered with circle metal letter stencils and hung from the bottom of tags for a title.

Heritage Photo Box, *Erikia Ghumm*

Travel Album, *Erikia Ghumm*

Adore, *Pamela Frye Hauer*

Dog Tags, *Emily Curry Hitchingham*

Her Tender Heart, *Erikia Ghumm*

TAGS *reinvented* 65

photographic tags

Photographs are a major component in scrapbooking and come in a wide range of formats. In addition to impacting how they look, the subject, composition, color and age of photos are also affected depending upon their form. This makes the possibilities for photos as a tag material almost endless. They may be cut into any shape and adorned with a wide variety of materials and techniques. Just keep in mind that it is advisable to use reproductions, as using originals is very likely to destroy their historical value.

Some of the formats that photographs come in can be quite unusual and may sometimes appear to be less than desirable for creating stellar scrapbook layouts. Don't hide these types of photographs in a shoe box. Have them take center stage by turning them into tags like the ones featured on this page, which simply use spiral paper clips and ribbon to complete the transformation. The addition of other odd materials and patterns plays up the quirky tags and fun theme of the layout.

Photos: *Dennis Eriksen*

Materials list: *Polaroid photographs, metal words, spiral paper clips, ribbon, foam spacers, scissors*

Denver 1993, *Erikia Ghumm*

Digital Beauty, *Sarah Fishburn*

Sunshine, *Erikia Ghumm*

Inspire, Achieve, Embrace, *Rhonda Solomon for Pixie Press*

Effusion, *Marah Johnson*

Sunshine Photographs printed onto a transparency sheet layered with vellum and printed papers create a unique tag. **Denver 1993** A special photo is showcased by adhering it to cardstock, cutting it into a tag and adorning it with simplistic embellishments. **Digital Beauty** A photographic collage is printed with assembled items using a scanner. **Effusion** More than one photograph is featured on a tag using tiny contact prints. **Imagine, Achieve, Embrace** Individual images are cut from one photograph to create several smaller photographs.

plastic t a g s

With all of its variations, plastic brings a unique twist to tag making. Everything from jewels and rhinestones that add a bit of shimmer, buttons and rulers with their domestic charm, to boldly shaped acrylic tags and playing cards make the creative possibilities practically endless. Plastic tags and embellishments can be found everywhere, from that odd junk drawer to a local scrapbook store. All plastic requires is a bit of creative thinking. One thing to keep in mind when creating with plastic is that not all types are of archival quality. When using plastic in scrapbooks, work with duplicate photographs or use the plastic tags or embellishments on other memory craft items such as album covers, wall art or projects such as greeting cards.

Materials list: *Plastic tags, cardstock letter stickers, engraving tool and soft cloth*

The engraved plastic tag title featured on this modern collage spread is a perfect material to play out the comical tone set by the photographs. Notice that the tags are layered over patterned paper, giving them additional interest. Other upbeat elements include the use of mesh, brightly colored printed and handmade papers and stamped embossed lips. The entire design is pulled together with stamping-ink accents.

Honey-Do, *Jodi Amidei*

School Days Album, *Erikia Ghumm*

1 Apply an individual letter sticker to a plastic tag, making sure it is well adhered. Using an engraving tool, outline the letter, working up to its edge to get a crisp image.

2 Once the letter is outlined, roughly engrave the surrounding surface, leaving a small un-engraved area along the outside edge of the tag.

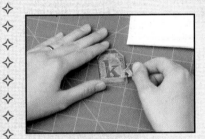

3 Remove the letter sticker and any dust.

School Days Album An album cover is embellished with an altered plastic ruler tag layered with letter stickers and printed paper. **Play** A whimsical tag created from plastic playing cards is embellished with dimensional items. **Oh Friend O' My Life** A funky, feminine tag is glamorized with chunky plastic rhinestone jewels and printed transparencies. **Treasure** White plastic buttons in vintage designs and antique doilies adorn this shabby chic tag. **Honey-Do** A plastic tag is stamped with solvent stamping ink and embellished with loose sparkling glitter adhered with spray adhesive and edged with a metallic paint pen.

Play, *Torrey Miller*

Oh Friend O' My Life,
Kelly Angard

Treasure, *Jennifer Bertsch*

polymer clay tags

Polymer clay has the ability to be turned into completely original tags and embellishments unlike any other substance. It comes in a variety of colors and textures and is relatively inexpensive. The most amazing thing about polymer clay is that you do not have to be a sculptor to create with it. There are several different tools to help with the formation of eye-catching clay adornments. An old rolling pin or retired pasta machine make the job of conditioning and flattening clay quick and easy. Shaped pieces can be fashioned effortlessly with old cookie cutters or templates and a clay knife. Textured or image-adorned pieces are instantly formed using rubber stamps. For the creation of 3-D pieces, there are various styles of soft rubber push molds, which are a cinch to use.

Photos: *Sheri Fain and Erikia Ghumm*

Faux stone tags are a perfect element to add to a tranquil scrapbook spread featuring springtime cemetery photographs. The secret to accomplishing the realistic look of weathered carved stone is through the use of simulated stone polymer clay and micaceous iron oxide acrylic paint. The paint contains tiny ground sparkling particles which helps to simulate the look of real stone. To carry the stone look throughout the design, it is repeated in other elements such as the crackle and stone architectural printed papers and the printed transparencies of statues and carved signs.

Materials list: *Simulated stone polymer clay, micaceous iron oxide or black acrylic paint, various stamps, a soft rubber push mold, rolling pin or clay-dedicated pasta machine, a hard nonporous work surface such as a piece of tile, clay tools, squirt bottle and container with water and a sponge*

Polymer Hanging Tag A tag is personalized with rubber stamps, acrylic paint and iridescent pigment powders and strung on a length of ribbon for hanging. **Voyage** Handmade letter "tiles" made with polymer clay, alphabet stamps and metallic paint make for an eye-catching tag title. **Home Sweet Home** Photocopied photographs are transferred onto polymer clay and are detailed with colored embossing powders. **Dream, Hope, Wonder** Hand-sculpted rose embellishments are adhered to a tag with strong silicone adhesive.

1 To create the flat medallion tags, condition a small piece of polymer clay by kneading it until it becomes pliable. Roll out the clay into a thin sheet using a rolling pin or clay-dedicated pasta machine. Working with a slightly water-moistened stamp, firmly push it into the clay, transferring the image. Cut out stamped images and make a small hole near the edge for adding ribbon. Repeat for additional tags.

2 Use the scraps left over from the creation of the flat medallion tags to create the dimensional "carved" flower tag elements. Start by prepping the soft rubber push mold by spritzing it with water. Roll small pieces of clay together and press into mold. Once the mold is filled, simply press the clay out from the backside to release it. Repeat for additional pieces.

3 Apply the iron oxide or black acrylic paint to the individual clay pieces using a sponge, working it into all of the crevices. Before the paint dries, wipe off the excess on the surface with a damp sponge until the desired look is achieved. Repeat on all clay pieces.

Polymer Hanging Tag, *Tricia Rubens*

Home Sweet Home,
Andrea Lyn Vetten-Marley

Tip: Keep in mind that any tools used in the creation of polymer clay embellishments should never be used for food preparation or storage.

Dream, Hope, Wonder,
Kerry Arquette

dream
hope
wonder

Travel *voyage*

Voyage, *Marah Johnson*

ribbon tags

When ribbon is used in the creation of tag art, it is typically tied through the hole in a tag to give it a finished look. However when ribbon is used as a tag material, it takes on a very different function and turns into an extravagant embellishment. Ribbon comes in countless colors, sizes, patterns and textures, making the choices for using it as a tag material endless. Moreover, because there are so many options when working with ribbon, most any style or theme can easily be achieved. Turning a length of ribbon into a tag can be as simple as adding an eyelet to one end or as involved as weaving several lengths together to create an exquisite tags base.

Materials list: *Various ribbons, sewing machine and scissors*

Various ribbons in coordinating colors are quickly turned into tags by folding over a few inches on the tops of each and securing the loops with stitching. The ribbon tags are attached to this high-fashion spread by sliding them over an old belt, which is then attached to the layout with strong foam adhesive. Additional embellishments round out the retro couture theme, including vintage clothing and accessories such as buttons, woven labels and metal logos. Dime store photo-booth photographs featuring the young beauty have been reprinted using a home computer.

She's Happy,
Erikia Ghumm

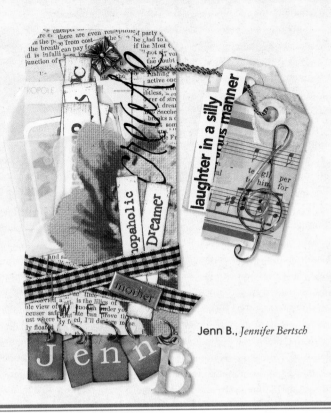

laughter in a silly
manner

Jenn B., *Jennifer Bertsch*

She's Happy Layers of sheer ribbon are adhered together with solid sheet adhesive, die cut and embellished with paper images and glitter glue. **My Love** A collaged tag is adorned with tied ribbon accents. **Madeline** Printed and stamped ribbons add stylish sentiments to tags. **Jenn B**. A ribbon wrapped around a tag is used as both a form of attachment and visual anchor for a collage. **Mom** Several different types of ribbon are woven together, trimmed, adhered to the tag base and then adorned with dimensional embellishments.

Madeline, *Marah Johnson*

My Love, *Marah Johnson*

Mom, *Tricia Rubens*

shaped metal-rimmed tags

Decorative shaped metal-rimmed tags are a whimsical spinoff of circle metal-rimmed tags. They come in several shapes and sizes and can be made from sturdy cardstock or vellum, which provide additional creative options. Almost any technique that can be applied to cardstock or vellum can be applied to these tags. Moreover, because their edges are sturdy, decorative shaped metal-rimmed tags are great to use on album covers and 3-D assemblages.

Some decorative shaped metal-rimmed tags have two rims that can be separated. Separating the rims is easy and can yield several creative possibilities. Like the tags featured on this page, they may be used to highlight journaling, particular words and different creative accents. Complete the tags with a snippet of ribbon.

Photos: *Brian Ghumm*

Materials list: *Shaped metal-rimmed tags, printed paper with journaling, mini foam adhesive, ribbon, 1/8" hole punch, scissors or craft knife with cutting mat*

Heaven Sent, *Erikia Ghumm*

1 Remove the metal rim from the tag by separating the layers with your fingers and peeling them apart. If it is difficult to get started, use the tip of a craft knife to start the separation.

2 Add printed journaling to the surface of the tag. Reattach the rim of the tag with mini foam adhesive and trim off any excess remaining outside the rim.

Amour, Amour!, *Erikia Ghumm*

3 Enhance the tag further with stamping ink stippled over the surface and glitter glue applied around the edges. Finish the tag with ribbon.

Photo Shoot, *Erikia Ghumm*

Flower Bouquet, *Erikia Ghumm*

Tasha, *Erikia Ghumm*

Amour, Amour! A piece of wall art is adorned with shaped metal-rimmed tags hung from a mini eye hook. **Heaven Sent** Printed transparencies are attached to a tag with metal tape to mimic the appearance of a metal rim. **Flower Bouquet** The style of flower-shaped metal-rimmed tags directs the theme for die-cut embellishments. **Photo Shoot** Personalized metal-rimmed tags are created with the application of metal tape to the edges of die cuts. **Tasha** A shaped metal-rimmed tag is modified by removing its edge, reapplying it over a photograph and trimming the excess.

shrink plastic tags

Shrink plastic has been used by rubber stampers and altered artists for many years to create sturdy, one-of-a-kind embellishments. It is a unique material that can be colored, stamped, cut and then heated, which causes it to shrink to about half of its original size. The shrinking process also thickens the plastic and sharpens the color and designs applied to it. There are various types of shrink plastic, including sanded, non-sanded and inkjet compatible. It is available in translucent, white, cream, brown and black varieties. Surfaces can be colored with inks, craft markers, colored pencils and chalks. Once shrunk down and while still warm, shrink plastic can be textured with stamps, left slightly curled, or flattened completely. Cutting shrink plastic is a cinch with a pair of old scissors, punches or a die-cut machine. With all of its fabulous attributes, shrink plastic accents make for dynamic personal embellishments.

Materials list: Tag die-cut shrink plastic, tag die-cut machine or templates, heat-set dye and pigment inks, letter and various image stamps, heat tool or toaster oven, heat-resistant surface, strong double-sided adhesive, ribbon, fibers and scissors

The shadows cast on the pastel-colored buildings in these photographs create a dark and mysterious feeling. Offset this mood with a bright shrink plastic tag title accented with soft ribbon and copper ties to give the layout energy. By using scrap photographs left over from a previous project, several photographs fit onto the three 7¼ x 7¼" pages.

Wish Upon a Star Die-cut shrink plastic colorized with paint pens makes for a one-of-a-kind embellishment. **She's So Nutty** Images stamped onto small shrink plastic tags create personalized charms. **Her Jewel-Tone Heart** Texture is added to shrink plastic pieces by stamping into them immediately after shrinking and then accentuating their raised designs with acrylic paints. **Memories** Shrink plastic was free-form cut into a tag, stamped with words and images, shrunk and colorized with alcohol inks. **Go With Your Heart** Cut, stamped and heat-shrunk plastic is enhanced with embossing powders.

Memories, *Tricia Rubens*

She's So Nutty, *Erikia Ghumm*

Wish Upon a Star,
Erikia Ghumm

Go With Your Heart, *Melissa Smith*

Her Jewel-Tone Heart, *Erikia Ghumm*

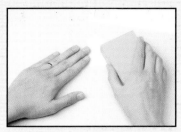

1 Gather as many tags needed to create a title. Remove them from a manufactured die-cut sheet of shrink plastic or cut tags from a sheet of shrink plastic using a die-cut machine or a pair of old scissors. Lightly sand both sides of the tags using a very fine grit sanding block to prevent the plastic from sticking to itself when heated.

2 Add heat-set stamping ink directly to one side of the tags along with stamped images of clocks, text and postage stamps. Stamp title using alphabet stamps. If a mistake is made, quickly clean off the inks with stamp cleaner and try again.

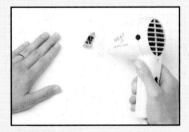

3 Working with one tag at a time, shrink using a heat tool on a heat- resistant surface such as a thick pad of paper. Unlike the heat tool shown here, some blow too much air and would require a tool to hold the tag down while it is being shrunk. The tag will curl up as it shrinks and when it is finished shrinking, it will flatten out. Just after heating, compress with a thick, flat object to completely flatten. Adorn with silk ribbon and fibers.

slide mount tags

Several decades ago, many families enjoyed their photographs not in scrapbooks, but as slide shows viewed upon a large screen. The life-size images that were produced were created from tiny transparent pictures framed within a paper or plastic slide mount. Slide mounts served this one purpose until they made their way into scrapbooking, where they are used in countless ways. They make delightful embellishments and lend themselves to many creative options, particularly as tags. Most plastic and paper varieties come in one size and color, but they are easily adorned using a plethora of materials and techniques. In addition, specialty slide mounts are available in different sizes and are printed with various images.

Photos: *Pamela Frye Hauer and Erikia Ghumm*

Materials list: *Plastic slide mounts in various colors, high-speed rotary tool with drill bit, eyelets, eyelet-setting tool, hammer and a block of wood to work on*

Decorative paper and simplistic plastic slide mounts create the ultimate tags for featuring photographs of a tacky state plate collection. This kitschy spread utilizes collaged map-print paper to convey a cheery travel theme. Although the printed paper is bursting with images and several colors, the spread remains orderly with graphic placement of the layout elements. Journaling cards are cleverly stored in the decorated library pocket and detail how the collection was started and where it currently stands, which can be updated as the collection grows.

Glamour Girl, *Kari Hansen-Daffin*

Miss. Ferne 1920's,
Erikia Ghumm

1 Working over a block of wood, drill a small hole close to the top and center of the plastic slide mount using a high-speed rotary tool with a drill bit. Do not apply too much pressure when drilling, as this might break the slide mount or the delicate drill bit.

2 Carefully set a regular eyelet into the drilled hole by gently tapping the setting tool with a hammer. Do not set the eyelet completely, as this may cause the plastic to crack.

Miss Ferne 1920s Slide mounts are transformed into mini picture frame showcasing a transparency photograph and pressed flowers sealed in laminate. **Doc and Gert Laugh** Stamps, paint pens and dimensional embellishments enhance an ordinary slide mount. **Indy** Adorned slide mounts are layered on top of each other for added depth. **Glamour Girl** Slide mounts are personalized when covered with printed papers matching the theme of the tag. **Boyhood** Stamped and inked paper slide mounts are incorporated into a collaged tag with stitching and paper clips.

Indy, *Janetta Wieneke*

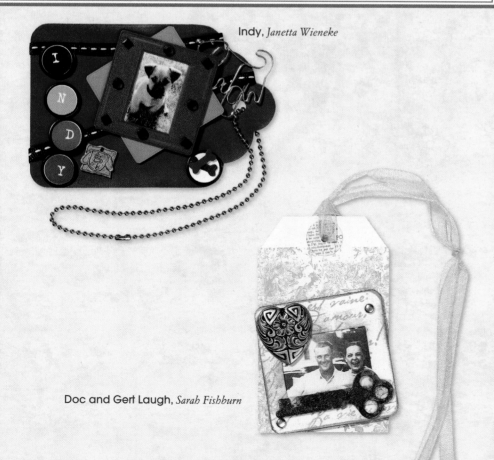

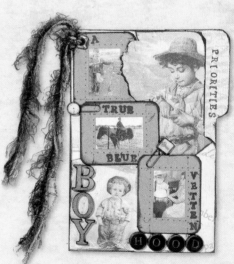

Boyhood, *Andrea Lyn Vetten-Marley*

Doc and Gert Laugh, *Sarah Fishburn*

sticker t a g s

Stickers come in a variety of sizes, shapes, colors, textures and designs. They are easy to work with and make an excellent tag material. Tag-shaped stickers and other sticker forms can be turned into sensational tag embellishments in a snap. Try using a variety of colorants such as inks, acrylic paints and embossing powders to change their appearance. Dimension may be added to stickers with beads, modeling paste and dimensional glaze. Combine these ideas with techniques such as stamping and collage and soon you will have a one-of-a-kind look that was deceptively easy to achieve.

This charming garden-themed spread uses sticker tags in two unique ways. The left side of the spread features mini tag-shaped stickers as photo mats. The right side of the spread features a sticker collage tag. Dimensional interest is added to all of the tags with brads that have been heat embossed with gold powder. This subtle detail ties the different tags together.

Materials List: *Printed textured stickers, shipping tag, water-based dye ink in spray bottle, heat tool and a large sheet of scrap paper*

Accomplishment, Appreciation,
Perseverance, *Terri Zwicker*

Journey, *Jennifer Bertsch*

Family Game Night, *Miki Benedict*

1 Tear stickers into random pieces
and apply them to a shipping tag,
leaving a few areas of the tag exposed.
Trim off any excess with scissors.

2 Working over a large piece of
scrap paper, spray the tag with
water-based dye ink until the desired
effect is achieved.

3 Heat-set the ink until it appears
dried and has a matte finish.

Eclectic, *Marah Johnson*

Adore, *Erikia Ghumm*

Adore Several different types of stickers are layered together to comprise
a collage tag. **Eclectic** Letter stickers forming a title are accentuated with
clear epoxy stickers. **Accomplishment, Appreciation, Perseverance**
Image and words stickers provide embellishments for tags and twill tape.
Journey A tag is layered with themed stickers and rub-on words. **Family
Game Night** Several different styles of letter stickers are combined for a
diverse look.

transparency t a g s

Transparencies can add a sophisticated, layered collage look to even the simplest of materials such as tags. They are manufactured in sheet form and are available in different patterns and colors. Transparencies can be created on a home computer, may be derived from photographic negative strips and may be altered with paints, stamping inks and cut, punched and die-cut into several shapes. Try attaching transparencies with brads, eyelets, staples, photo corners and solid sheet adhesive. With all of the techniques that can be applied to transparencies, they offer a multitude of creative possibilities.

Photos: *Brian and Erikia Ghumm*

The transparency tags featured on this altered book layout are used in a number of ways to create a diverse, layered look. The largest tag is a preprinted die-cut transparency used as a photo mat. The title "Poipu" is a combination of stamped shipping tags covered with colored transparency sheets while "Beach" is a photographic negative strip adorned with vellum letter stickers.

Materials list: *Printed sheet and tag transparencies, mini shipping tags, stamping inks, alphabet stamps, acrylic paints, paintbrush, Xyron or solid sheet adhesive, scissors or craft knife, ruler and cutting mat*

Blue A tag is layered with printed transparencies, colorized with iridescent acrylic paints and stamped with a word using solvent stamping ink. **Twenty Carat** A layered illusion is achieved by placing word-printed transparencies on top of a collaged tag. **Game of Life** Images cut from printed transparencies are adhered to printed papers to create a personalized design. **Mystery** An otherwise plain bingo card is artfully enhanced with printed transparencies. **1953** Printed transparencies attached over fabric promote a distinctive textured look.

Mystery, *Marah Johnson*

Blue, *Cherie Ward*

1 Highlight various areas of the preprinted, die-cut transparency tag with acrylic paint on the backside. Use a dry brush technique with very little paint to give the painted highlights a timeworn look.

2 Stamp title onto mini shipping tags using unmounted alphabet stamps and acrylic blocks for easy centering of the letters. Colorize the edges of each tag by wiping them across the surface of an ink pad.

3 Apply a layer of solid adhesive to the transparencies using an adhesive-application machine or sheet adhesive. Layer over the stamped shipping tags and the photo backed with printed cardstock. Trim off any excess.

Game of Life, *Pamela Frye Hauer*

1953, *Marah Johnson*

Twenty Carat, *Sarah Fishburn*

ultra thick embossing powder tags

Ultra thick embossing powder is a large particle resin that is comparable to regular embossing powder. The two can be used in similar ways but produce different effects. When melted, a dimensional finish more substantial than regular embossing powder is created, allowing for more creative possibilities. One coat produces a bumpy "linoleum" finish and several coats produce a smooth "glasslike" finish. Using ultra thick embossing powder to embellish tags opens the door to a plethora of artistic options. Try using it to cover an entire tag, apply it to a bold stamped image for an irregular rendition, use it to highlight select images, or stamp into the warm substance for ultimate texture.

Ultra thick embossing powder is used in a number of ways to embellish the tags on this spread. The tags with letters "K," "N" and "V" are completely covered with three coats, creating a smooth finish. The tags with letters "E" and "I" are made with bold alphabet stamps and one application of black ultra thick embossing powder. The remaining tags are highlighted with clear or pearl-colored ultra thick embossing powder for a textured effect along with various other elements that tie the spread together.

Materials list: *Clear ultra thick embossing powder, dye and embossing ink pads, various image stamps, foam-tipped blending tool, heat tool, alphabet stencil, thick pad of paper or other heat-resistant work surface*

Photos: *Brian Ghumm*

Imagine, *Erikia Ghumm*

Observation, *Terri Zwicker*

1 Stamp text design onto an alphabet stencil. Colorize the edges of the stencil with dye stamping ink and a foam-tipped blending tool.

2 Cover the entire surface of the stencil with embossing ink by wiping the ink pad over its surface. Next, coat the wet stencil with clear ultra thick embossing powder.

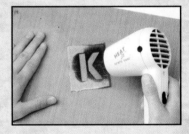

3 Working over a heat-resistant surface, heat the ultra thick embossing powder until it has melted. If a smooth finish is desired, apply additional coats of embossing ink and ultra thick embossing powder.

Kirk and Roo Applying one layer of dark ultra thick embossing powder over a chipboard tag gives it a bumpy finish which is further embellished using dimensional accents applied with foam adhesive. **Imagine** A butterfly die-cut is highlighted with several applications of ultra thick embossing powder and glitter. **Just Married** Pressed flowers and plastic opalescent chips are suspended within layers of ultra thick embossing powder. **In This Joyful and Happy Hour...** A slide mount is given added visual interest with coats of ultra thick embossing powder that were cracked through bending after the material cooled. **Observation** Collaged printed paper elements and stamped images are covered with clear ultra thick embossing powder.

Just Married, *Erikia Ghumm*

Kirk and Roo, *Erikia Ghumm*

In This Joyful and Happy Hour...,
Marah Johnson

TAGS *reinvented* 85

vintage emphemera t a g s

Vintage ephemera is similar to modern ephemera in that it consists of paper items that were designed to be short-lived. In past eras, people often saved everything from scraps of wrapping paper, greeting cards, matchbooks, paper coasters and other items that could be reused or that held personal significance. Consequently, it is relatively easy to find pieces of vintage ephemera at antique shops, flea markets, garage sales, online auction sites and Internet shops at reasonable prices. Another great way to economically amass a collection is to ask family and friends if they have any such items they would be willing to part with. Like modern ephemera, vintage ephemera is typically not archivally sound. However, pieces can be printed onto archival paper using a scanner and printer or copy machine, sealed with laminate, or misted with an acid-neutralizer and UV inhibitor. In addition, there are several manufacturers that offer beautiful reproductions intended for scrapbooking.

Materials list: *Various pieces of vintage ephemera, printed transparency, Xyron machine or other type of solid sheet adhesive, corner rounder, hole punch, scissors, paper trimmer or ruler, craft knife and cutting mat*

Combining different aged and modern materials gives this sweet and colorful baby shower layout an eclectic look. The element that ties the pieces together is the whimsical vintage ephemera tag. It was created with an image of a stork and baby cut from retro wrapping paper, which was adhered to an old book page and layered with a graphic printed transparency. The transparency was flawlessly adhered using a solid adhesive applied with a Xyron machine. The tag was then adorned with a ticket and eyelet topper of torn silk ribbon. The words "Pam's Baby Shower" were created by running thin cardstock strips through an office label maker and accentuating with stamping inks.

Cool Fridges, *Kari Hansen-Daffin*

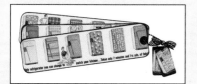

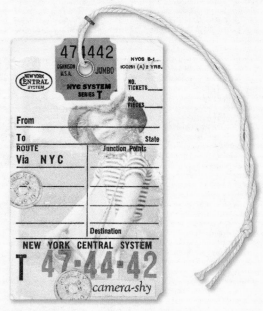

Camera Shy, *Sarah Fishburn*

French Fashion, *Trisha McCarty-Luedke*

So Perfect, *Erikia Ghumm*

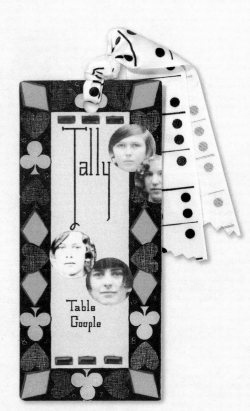

Tally, *Sarah Fishburn*

So Perfect Printed reproduction ephemera is die cut into a tag and adorned with various elements. **Camera Shy** A reproduction photograph is transferred onto a vintage ephemera tag. **Tally** Vintage ephemera is layered with photographs and 3-D embellishments. **Cool Fridges** Images clipped from vintage magazines and books are adhered to a cardstock tag. **French Fashion** Handmade and reproduction pieces comprise an inspired tag.

wood tags

With its earthy color and texture, wood is unlike any other material and is marvelous to use for creating tags. Wood tags are manufactured in a variety of colors and numerous shapes, sizes and thicknesses. In addition to using actual die-cut wood tags, look to incorporate other unique items such as craft sticks, chopsticks and balsawood pieces. While the creative possibilities are endless, keep in mind that wood is not acid- and lignin-free. If this is a concern, printed and coated wood papers provide attractive alternatives that will be safe for your scrapbooks.

Materials list: *Wood tags, sticker and real pressed flowers, ground mica flakes, walnut ink in spray bottle, acrylic adhesive or decoupage glaze, paintbrush, scratch and waxed paper*

The nature-inspired, "hippie era" theme of this scrapbook spread is reflected in the use of natural wood tags. The tags are adorned with sticker and real pressed flowers combined with a hint of shimmering ground mica. Paired with colorful printed and handcolored papers, faux engraved rocks, stitching and calligraphy stickers, these tags are natural choices for page accents and are reminiscent of handmade items of the time.

Photos: *Dennis Eriksen*

Their Good-Bye Wood craft sticks are decoupaged with paper imagery and printed papers and are hung with a miniature ball chain through drilled holes. **Parrot Brand Oranges** A wood veneer tag is simply embellished, enabling its natural beauty to shine through. **Luca** A personalized tag frame complete with title is created using wood veneer sheets and wood letters. **Gold Kissed Foliage** Designs are hand-drawn onto wood tags then carved and enhanced with acrylic paints, walnut ink and embossing powders. **Discover the Journey** A hobby iron is used to accentuate a wood tag by burning a word into its surface, which is then embellished with other natural elements.

1 Working over a scratch piece of paper, spray wood tags lightly with walnut ink. If a darker color is desired, repeat the application.

2 Add pressed flower stickers and real pressed flowers adhered with an acrylic adhesive. Apply one coat of adhesive to the decorated tags to seal their surface.

3 While the adhesive is still wet, sprinkle the tags with ground mica flakes for a natural sparkle.

Their Good Bye, *Erikia Ghumm*

Luca, *Andrea Zocchi*

Parrot Brand Oranges, *Erikia Ghumm*

Gold Kissed Foliage, *Torrey Miller*

Discover the Journey, *Tricia Rubens*

Supplies and Credits

Page 6
Tag Art Experiments
Erikia Ghumm
Photo: Ken Trujillo
Sewing printed cardstocks and tag, black twill tape with eyelets, printers type stickers, decorative safety pins (Club Scrap), velvet leaves, reproduction paper, fabric photographs and postcards, copper charm (ARTchix Studio), sliver glitter glue (Ranger), optometrist lens, yellow domino, scrabble tiles (Limited Edition), black text printed paper, printed twist tie (Pebbles), reproduction bird ephemera, (Me & My Big Ideas), red star brad, heart and square epoxy stickers (Creative Imaginations), brass safety pin, large antique brass eyelet (Prym-Dritz), alphabet stencils (Ma Vinci's Reliquary), pink plastic tag (KI Memories), gold leafing (USArtQuest), copper mesh (AMACO), blue butterfly (Design Originals), black fiber (Art Sanctum), playing card, black dot fabric, chandelier crystal, heart pet identification tag, black cameo, can lid, threads, acrylic paint, oil pastels, purple and green fibers, maroon, red, leopard and gingham ribbons, mini orange, red and white ribbons, silver and purple eyelets, black dye ink, plum, lime and orange spray dye inks, transparency, vintage words cut from book and book page, snap ephemera, key, bottle cap, rhinestone broach, green pearls, handmade plum, lime and orange papers

Pages 12-13 Album Tags
Beauty Queen
Album, photo corners (Kolo) large alphabet stamps (Ma Vinci's Reliquary), small alphabet stamps (Hero Arts), glitter glue (Ranger), original, reproduction vintage labels (Limited Edition), ink jet photo paper (Epson), labels (Dymo), epoxy hole reinforcements (EK Success) colored glittered bobby pins, ribbon, rhinestones, stamping ink

Soul Mates
Mini scrapbook, stickers (Creative Imaginations), alphabet stamps (Hero Arts), silk flower (Michaels), eyelets, rhinestones, ribbon, stamping inks

"Younique" Women
Binding discs, clear plastic cover, binding punch (Rollabind), shipping tags (American Tag Co.) "younique" sticker, epoxy letter stickers (Creative Imaginations), trims (vintage), ribbon

Born on the 4th of July
Small file folders (Paper Adventures), 3-D stickers (EK Success), wooden letters, marine emblem, postage (Li'l Davis Designs), stickers (Sticker Studio, Pebbles, Karen Foster Design, Me & My Big Ideas), metal letters (Making Memories), star charm (Magic Scraps), printed papers (Rusty Pickle), pigment stampin' ink

Beauty
Printed paper (Design Originals), die-cut (Sherenshnitte Designs), rub-ons, metal mesh (Making Memories), fabric Labels (Me & My Big Ideas), printed epoxy stickers (Creative Imaginations), jump rings (Westrim), floral Sticker (EK Success), velvet leaves, fabric (unknown)

It's Random
Tag album, mini glass bottle (7 Gypsies), decorative stamp, rub-on letters (Making Memories), acrylic paint, ribbons, charms

Pages 14-15 Alphabet Stencil Tags
A Life Altering Event
Printed papers, faux metal and letter stickers (Sticker Studio), album, mini tag, cardstock (DMD), alphabet stamps and stencils (Ma Vinci's Reliquary), library pocket, mini eyelets (Limited Edition), mini alphabet stamps (Hero Arts), faux rust paint kit (Delta), negative strips (Creative Imaginations), printed artist's tape (Club Scrap), gel medium for photo transfers (Golden Artist Colors), walnut ink (7 Gypsies), metal tag (Chronicle Books), index tab (Z-International), paper clips, waxed twine (unknown), ribbon

Smile
Printed alphabet stencil (Autumn Leaves), cardstock (DMD), acrylic paint, ribbon, paper clip

Howdy
Stencil (US Stamp and Sign), Jute (Natures Handmade), patterned paper (Flair Designs), eyelet

Fun with Letters
Vintage lettering stencil (Stenso CO.), printed paper (Design Originals), square conchos, mini alphabet stencils (Scrapworks), ribbon, marker

Japanese "K"
Japanese geisha and coin stamps (Stamp Magick), Chinese calligraphy stamp (All Night Media), gold embossing powder (Ranger), red printed paper (Print Blocks), Mizuhiki cord (Yasumoto), ribbon, pigment stamping ink

Dad
Foam core (Magic Scraps), leather paper (K & Company), tag template, paper (Provo Craft), metal circle stencil (Scrapworks), decorative brads, metal phrase (Making Memories), watch parts (unknown)

Pages 16-17 Beaded Tags
Until the End of Time
Printed papers, postage stamp stickers (Scrappy Cat Creations), seed bead mix, nailhead numbers (JewelCraft), saying stickers, decorative eyelet (Creative Imaginations), letter stamps (Ma Vinci's Reliquary), clock, "time" stamp (Limited Edition), pearl pigment powder (Ranger), ink jet photo paper (Epson), tag die-cut, photo corners (Sizzix), alphabet beads (Create A Craft), album (Mrs. Grossman's), green ribbon, black ink

Life is a Gamble
Mat board (Hobby Lobby), reproduction photo (ARTchix Studio), swirl stamp (Stampin' Up!), metallic paint pen (Ranger), sheet adhesive (Xyron), gel medium sealant (Golden Artist Colors), beads (Blue Moon Beads), book page, playing cards (vintage) circle metal-rimmed tag (Z-International), handmade tag, ribbon, wire, stamping ink

Memories
Printed tag with silk tassel (Me & My Big Ideas), tiny glass marbles (Magic Scraps)

Imagination
Chipboard tag, image of girl (DMD), bead "paint" (Deco Arts), metal spiral (7 Gypsies) "Imagination" stamp (Limited Edition), stamping ink, ribbon, fibers

Four Girls and Their Horse
Tiny postcards, decorative paper clip, 3-D typewriter keys, hole reinforcement (EK Success), printed paper (Me & My Big Ideas), handmade tag, ribbon, fibers

Merry Christmas
Photographic stickers (Pebbles Inc.), printed die-cuts (Doodlebug Design), puzzle punch (EK Success), beaded wire (Wal-Mart), tree eyelet (Carolee's Creations), fibers

Pages 18-19 Bottle Cap Tags
Squirt
Light blue wood printed paper, letter stickers (Pebbles), (Creative Imaginations), cardstock, colored ball chain (Club Scrap), "Precious" and "Love" bottle caps (Li'l Davis Designs), dark blue crackle printed paper (Me & My Big Ideas), ink jet photo paper (Epson), photo corner punch (EK Success), handmade mini circle stamp, stamping ink, acrylic paint, vintage soda bottle caps

Bathing Beauty
Image of woman (ARTchix Studio), glitter glue (Ranger), alphabet stamps (Hero Arts), circle epoxy sticker (Creative Imaginations), ribbon, stamping ink, bottle cap, chandelier crystal, glass jar

Adore Siblings Album
Binding discs, clear plastic cover, binding punch (Rollabind), cardstock (DMD), shipping tag (American Tag Co.), ink jet photo paper (Epson), "Adore" bottle cap (Li'l Davis Designs), dye stamping ink and glitter glue (Ranger), alphabet stamps (Ma Vinci's Reliquary), date stamp (unknown), label maker (Dymo), vintage fabric, rickrack, thread, ribbon

Ann Hall 1936
Cardstock (DMD), printed transparency (Magic Scraps), cyanotype paper (Nature Print Paper), velvet leaves (ARTchix Studio), mesh (AMACO), flower punch (Emagination Crafts), brad (American Tag Co.), bottle cap, ribbon, acrylic paint, paper clip

Fun at the Amusement Park
Bottle caps (ARTchix Studio), "Road Trip" bottle cap (Li'l Davis Designs), flower brad (Making Memories), printed paper, ticket stickers (Karen Foster Design), circle mesh (Magic Mesh), square conchos, alphabet stencils (Scrapworks), ribbon, wire

God Bless America
Walnut-inked tags, silver square ring (Rusty Pickle), bottle caps (Jest Charming), metal mesh (Making Memories), ribbon, acrylic paint

Pages 20-21 Can Lid Tags
Grandmother
Printed papers, epoxy letter stickers (Creative Imaginations), cardstock (Club Scrap), can lids (Found), watch parts, spiral paper clip, silk ribbon (7 Gypsies), crackle stamp, dimensional glaze (JudiKins), fleur-de-lis stamps (Unknown), large alphabet stamps (Ma Vinci's Reliquary), small alphabet stamps (Hero Arts), labels (Dymo), glitter glue (Ranger), mesh (Magic Scraps), ink jet photo paper (Epson), gauze fabric (vintage), stamping ink, acrylic paint, silver pen

Photo Box 2003-2004
Photo box (Kolo), printed paper, date stamps (Making Memories), child with butterfly stamp (ARTchix Studio) solvent stamping ink (Tsukineko), can lid, ribbon

Delight
Butterfly embellishment, "delight" dimensional sticker, watch charm (K & Company), dimensional glaze (Ranger), ribbon, can lid, eyelets, wire

Sheri and Mother
Printed paper, flower sticker (K & Company), velvet leaves (ARTchix Studio), glitter glue (Ranger), cardstock (Club Scrap), calligraphy ink (Dr. Ph. Martin's)
Cabochon (JewelCraft), vintage button, ribbon, can lid, acrylic paint

USA
Mesh (Magic Mesh), patriotic stickers (Sticker Studio), label stickers (Pebbles Inc.), gold stars (ARTchix Studio), typewriter keys (Creative Imaginations), wire, can lids cut with Pampered Chef can opener

The Length of Life
Sunflower die-cut (Paper House Productions), printed paper (Rusty Pickle), Twigs (7 Gypsies), tiny glass marbles mixed into painted border (Magic Scraps), Altoid's can lid, ribbon

Pages 22-23 Canvas Tags
Souvenir Songs
Inkjet canvas, wood grain printed vellum, bamboo border stickers, epoxy letter and flower stickers (Creative Imaginations), red and white printed cardstock, vellum (Club Scrap), file folder (DMD), oil paints (Marshall's), labels (Dymo), raffia (Robin's Nest), ink jet photo paper (Epson), mini alphabet stamps (Hero Arts), index tab (Z-International), colored staples (Target), vintage sheet music clip art, red and green stamping inks

Happiness
Ink jet photo paper, starburst accent (Creative Imaginations), dark blue embossing powder (Ranger), mini brad (Karen Foster Design), colored paper clips (Wal-Mart), oil Cloth (unknown)

Sweet Flowers
Ink jet canvas, epoxy word stickers (Creative Imaginations), pansy image (vintage), gel medium (Golden Artist Colors), measuring tape sticker (K & Company), spiral paper clip (Cavallini and Co.)

Create your Dreams
Canvas tags, rub-on words (Creative Imaginations), square collage stamps (Limited Edition), black ball chain (Club Scrap), stamping ink, plastic closure and soda pop tabs

Delight
Canvas (Vintage Workshop), alcohol inks, mica (USArtQuest), pigment powder (Pearl Ex), printed twill ribbon (Creative Impressions), "delight" die-cuts (QuicKutz), gold extra thick embossing powder, embossing ink, acrylic paint, ribbon

Travel, Journey, Adventure
Acrylic glaze (Golden Artist Colors), postage stamp stickers (Me & My Big Ideas), mesh (Magic Mesh), printed twill (7 Gypsies), brads (Creative Impressions), compass (Magic Scraps), beaded trim (unknown), tan canvas, leather, denim, buckle, dictionary page, stamping ink

Pages 24-25 Cardstock Tags
Happiness
Printed and plain cardstocks, Asian imagery, script, and alphabet stamps, small Chinese coin, paper label holder, brads (Club Scrap), Asian shrink plastic symbol (Ranger), sheet adhesive (Xyron), ink jet watercolor photo paper (Epson), large Chinese script stamp (All Night Media), large Chinese coin (Stampington & Co.), labels (Dymo), silk tassel (American Tag Co.), Asian postage stamp (Toybox), stamping ink, embossing powder, fiber

B and E
Cardstock (DMD), tag die-cut (Sizzix), bird and script reproduction ephemera (Design Originals), "B&E" stamps (Hero Arts), date Stamp (Making Memories), dye stamping ink, inkjet photo paper (Epson), acrylic paint

Always Believe in Yourself
Cardstock (DMD) printed papers (Design Originals, Creative Imaginations), glitter (Magic Scraps), stamps (Clearsnap), woven label saying (Me & My Big Ideas), ink jet photo paper (Epson), labels (Dymo), nailhead (JewelCraft), plastic closure tab, pigment and stamping inks, ribbon

Sing, Dance, Delight
Dark green cardstock (DMD), light blue, pink and yellow cardstock (Bazzill), epoxy word and flower stickers (K & Company), flower punch (Emagination Crafts), leaf punch (Family Treasures) (unavailable), tags (handmade), dye stamping inks, ribbon, eyelets, skewers

Tree Top, Chinese Silk, Patti Jo
Vintage image (Roben-Marie Smith's), flower cutout (DMD), handmade cardstock paint chip, paint chip, double-sided ribbon, yellow highlighter

Fortune Cookie Flag Book
Printed and plain cardstocks, cardstock tags, label holder, chipboard, stamps (Club Scrap), fortunes, beads, fibers, dye stamping ink

Pages 26-27 Circle Metal-Rimmed Tags
Hunter Summer 2001
Printed papers (Paper Adventures, Magenta), mesh sheet (Magenta), rub-on tag backgrounds, letters "Hunter" (Creative Imaginations), tickets (Limited Edition), "Devotion", "Joy" stamps (Inkadinkado), "Summer 2001" stamp (Making Memories), spiral paper clip (Cavallini and Co.), dye stamping ink

2 Create
Circle album, (DMD),"2 Create" sticker (Creative Imaginations), copper circled-rimmed tag (EK Success), ribbon, acrylic paint, cardstock

Flower Seed Jar
Circle-rimmed tag (EK Success), printed seed transparency (K & Company), seed packed sticker (Limited Edition), cardstock (Club Scrap), glitter glue (Ranger), ribbon, acrylic paint, jar

Explosion of Laughter
Shipping and circle-rimmed tag (American Tag Co.), ink jet photo paper (Epson), glitter glue (Ranger) comics, ribbon

ABC Book
Circle-rimmed tags (DMD), letter stickers (Mrs. Grossman's), loose leaf paper ring (Office Max), alphabet solitaire game (Whiskey Creek)

Asian Invasion
Circle-rimmed cork tag (Creative Imaginations), patterned paper (Chatterbox), Asian face stamps (Stamp Magick), Chinese stamp (All Night Media), copper mini circle- rimmed tags (EK Success), paper fibers (Heart Strings), copper paint pen (Krylon)

Pages 28-29 CD Tags
Thru the Decades
Texture printed paper, epoxy words and letter stickers, rub-on words (Creative Imaginations), printed transparencies (Magic Scraps), "Memories", "Time", number, clock face stamps (Limited Edition), "Moments" definition stamp (Hero Arts), "Love" stamp (Inkadinkado), ink jet photo paper (Epson), black ribbon, diskette, CD, orange ribbon, solvent and dye stamping inks

Grab Happines
Saying sticker, printed paper (Club Scrap), printed transparency (Magic Scraps), inkjet canvas (Creative Imaginations), nailhead (Scrapworks), floppy disk, ribbon, staples, pigment and stamping inks, torn vintage book page

Time Keeps on Passing
Tag die-cut (Sizzix), teal paper (Paper Adventures), painted papers, hole reinforcement (Handmade), extra thick embossing powder (Ranger), "Time" and clock stamps (Limited Edition), printed clock face die-cut (DMD), metal watch face (Li'l Davis Designs), labels (Dymo), acrylic paint, CD, thread, stamping ink

Silent Screen
Printed paper (DMD), beads (Blue Moon Beads), CD, pigment stamping ink, ribbon

Cool
Alcohol inks (USArtQuest), glitter glue (Ranger), hole reinforcement sticker (Stampendous!), mini circle-rimmed tags, letter stickers (EK Success), silver paint pen (Krylon), CD

Boys Will Be Boys
Plastic mosaic pieces (Heidi Grace Designs), epoxy word stickers (Creative Imaginations), saying transparency (Design Originals), floppy disk, fibers

Pages 30-31 Cork Tags
In the Garden of Life
Album (Kolo), cork (Magic Scraps), flower, butterfly patterns (Colonial Patterns, Inc.), printed paper, transparency (K & Company), cardstock, mini tag (DMD), ink jet photo paper (Epson), nailheads (JewelCraft), photographic butterfly die-cut (Paper House Productions), vintage seed packet sticker (Art Accents), labels (Dymo), spiral paper clip, ribbon, stamping inks

Life's Little Lessons
Album (Kolo), square metal-rimmed cork tag (Creative Imaginations), postage stamp stickers (K & Company), glitter glue (Ranger), cancellation stamp (Hero Arts), vintage words cut from book, ribbon, brads, waxed twine, stamping ink

Artist's Motif No. 1
Velvet leaves, image of woman, fleur-de-lis charm (ARTchix Studio), shipping tag (American Tag Co.), square cork and epoxy stickers (Creative Imaginations), stamp (Clearsnap), alphabet stamps (Hero Arts), glitter glue (Duncan), ticket (Limited Edition), rose sticker (Paper House Productions), vintage words cut from book page, ribbon, staples, pigment stamping ink

Yahoo
Tag (Club Scrap), red brads (Limited Edition), wire horse (Karen Foster Design), cork letters (Lazerletterz), horse shoe punch (Punch Bunch), metallic rub-ons (Craf-T), denim, bandana, leather, brads, floss, dye stamping ink

The Simple Life
Cork (Creative Impressions), circle rimmed cork tags (Creative Imaginations), farm ephemera (DMD), clothes pins (7 Gypsies), die-cut letters (Quickutz), walnut ink (Fiber Scraps), wood paper (unknown), chicken wire, canvas, acrylic paint

Color and Texture
Printed paper (Daisy D's), cork letter stickers (Creative Imaginations), letter stickers (Pebbles), canvas paper (FiberMark), staples

Pages 32-33 Cyanotype Tags
Kauai
Printed paper, cardstock, die-cut tag (Club Scrap), Ink jet photo paper (Epson), cyanotype paper (Nature Print Paper), mesh (Magenta), large alphabet stamps (Ma Vinci's Reliquary), small alphabet stamps (Hero Arts), photo corners (Kolo), mini compass (Limited Edition), Hawaiian postage stamp (Art Accents), colored staples (Target), ribbon, stamping ink, vintage clothing scrap ribbon

Summer Field
Pretreated cyanotype paper (Nature Print Paper), tag (Sizzix), "Summer Field" (Paint chip), fiber, button

Key to my Heart
Cyanotype paper (Nature Print Paper), cardstock (DMD), typewriter key stamps, epoxy hole reinforcement, (EK Success), stamping ink, fibers

Family Heroes
Cyanotype paper (Nature Print Paper) reproduction ephemera, (Me & My Big Ideas), alphabet stamps (Hero Arts), crackle stamp (JudiKins), star brad, epoxy sticker (Creative Imaginations), die-cut photo corner (Sizzix), cardstock (DMD), paper clip, paint chip, fibers

Photographs Album
Album (Kolo), blue printed paper (Scrappy Cat Creations) heat stamp (Inkadinkado), "Photographs" stamp (Limited Edition), diamond stamp (Paper Candy), glitter glue (Ranger), vintage fabric, laminate chip, solvent ink

Cherish Memories
Cyanotype paper (Nature Print Paper), metal mesh, rub-on words (Making Memories), beads (Blue Moon Beads), faux stone spray paint (Krylon), floss

Pages 34-35 Die-Cut Tags
The Eriksen's Farm
Square printed paper, faux wax seal (Creative Imaginations), printed papers (Design Originals, Wordsworth), cardstock (DMD), photographic die-cuts (Paper House Productions), letter stamps (Hero Arts), circle punches (Family Treasures), ribbon, stamping ink

Wish You Were Here
Photographic suitcase die-cut (Paper House Productions), postage stamp stickers (Me & My Big Ideas), date stamp (Making Memories), ink jet photo paper (Epson), fibers, dye stamping ink

Congratulations
Library pocket and card (Limited Edition), dot stamps (Hero Arts), glitter glue (Ranger), photographic couple die-cut (Paper House Productions), nailhead, rhinestone (JewelCraft), woven label, (Me & My Big Ideas), photo corners (Kolo), handmade card, ribbon, pigment stamping ink

Grandma
Prism paper (Grafix), blue printed paper (Provo Craft), printed epoxy stickers (Creative Imaginations), "Grandma" sticker (Pebbles), star die-cut (Sizzix), ribbon

Summer
Printed accordion tag die-cut (DMD), dot printed paper (Deluxe Designs), printed transparencies (Magic Scraps), die-cut letters (Sizzix), charms (Scrap Arts), floss, pigment stamping ink

Girl Through Window
Die-cut window tag (DMD), vintage image of girl, die-cut flowers (unknown), vintage pink tassel

Pages 36-37 Embossed Paper Tags
A Deeper Love
Cardstock, mesh papers (Club Scrap), cardstock shipping tags (DMD), glitter glue (Ranger), die-cut and sticker butterflies (Paper House Productions), alphabet template (Wordsworth), embossed frame (K & Company), nailheads (JewelCraft), script stamp (Hero Arts), ink jet photo paper (Epson), photo corners (Canson), paint chip, words cut from vintage book, washers, fibers, dye stamping ink, acrylic paint

Amour
Embossed paper (K & Company), reproduction photograph and ephemera, (ARTchix Studio), faux wax seal, printed paper (Creative Imaginations), cardstock (DMD), labels (Dymo) handmade tag, silk ribbon

Lemonade
Tag, paper label holder, embossed lemon paper, colored ball chain (Club Scrap), fruit crate and juice labels (Limited Edition), light blue printed paper, brad rub-on, brad (Creative Imaginations), metallic pigment powders, glitter glue (Ranger), labels (Dymo), paper clip, dye stamping ink, soda pop tab

Got Style?
Embossed paper (FiberMark), photo negative (Creative Imaginations), letter Stickers (Pebbles), coin envelope (American Tag Co.), ribbon, fiber

Sweetness
Printed paper (7 Gypsies, Paper Company), mini brads (American Tag Co.), photo slides (Making Memories), black specialty paper (Metropolis Designs)

Focused
Handmade paper, printed paper (Creative Imaginations), tag (7 Gypsies), rubber stamps (Barnes & Noble), cardstock (National Cardstock), buttons, feathers, staples

Pages 38-39 Embossing Foil Tags
Personality
Printed papers, printed twist ties, word border, "R" and "E" stickers (Pebbles Inc.), red embossing foil (Amaco), bottle cap, epoxy stickers, rub-on letters (Creative Imaginations), alphabet stamps "AND" "APRIL" (Hero Arts), labels, (Dymo), postage stamp punch (EK Success), ink jet photo paper (Epson), dye stamping ink

Kauai Sea Glass Jar
Embossing foil (Amaco), beads (JewelCraft), circle punches (Emagination Crafts), alphabet stamps (Hero Arts), solvent stamping ink, wire, acrylic paint, spice jar, vintage cord

Imagine
"Imagine" letter die-cuts (QuicKutz), alcohol inks (Ranger), stamping ink, ribbon, metal tape, tags

USMC 1962
Tag template (Deluxe Designs), embossing foil (Amaco), steel alphabet stamps, eyelets (Making Memories), silver paint pen (Krylon), wire, chalk, solvent stamping ink

Be Yourself
Heavy gauge embossing foil (Making Memories), Star metal-rimmed tag, epoxy word stickers (Creative Imaginations), metal tag (Anima Designs), red and blue square acrylic tags (Heidi Grace Designs), prism paper (Grafix), vintage photograph (ARTchix Studio), dimensional glaze (JudiKins), letter stickers (Pebbles Inc.), negative strips, ribbon

Pages 40-41 Epoxy Stickers Tags
Golden Moments
Printed papers, epoxy tags and letter stickers, "treasure" wire word (Creative Imaginations), dictionary printed paper (Design Originals), gold leafing (Biblical Impressions), skeleton leaves (Arnold Grummer), leaf stamps (Hero Arts), crackle stamp (JudiKins), brass brads (Magic Scraps), copper brads (American Tag Co.), labels (Dymo), ribbon

Create Believe Imagine
Epoxy word stickers, faux wax seals (Creative Imaginations), cardstock (DMD), pigment ink, ribbon, handmade tag

First Class Letters
Mini file folder, printed papers, ephemera, mini envelope, watch face, cardstock (DMD), epoxy tag sticker (Creative Imaginations), "First Class" stamp (PSX Design), labels (Dymo), postage stamp (Toybox), dye stamping ink

Remember Family History
White printed epoxy word and letter stickers, conchos (Li'l Davis Designs), velvet leaves (ARTchix Studio), ink jet photo paper (Epson), 45 record, ribbon, vintage rhinestone brooch

Hugs and Kisses
Printed paper (7 Gypsies), photo negative (Creative Imaginations), word label stickers (Pebbles), photo slides (Making Memories), specialty paper (FiberMark), ribbon

Hold Me Tight
Epoxy tag stickers (Creative Imaginations), pressed flowers (Nature's Pressed), reproduction photograph transparencies (ARTchix Studio)

Pages 42-43 Fabric Tags
Hilde 1888-1972
Printed papers, butterfly and feather embellishments, "Grandma" sticker, reproduction ephemera (K & Company), inkjet iron-on transfer paper (Epson), alphabet stamps (Ma Vinci's Reliquary), velvet leaves (ARTchix Studio), walnut ink (Anima Designs), cardstock (Bazzill), vintage linen table cloth, handkerchief, lace, straight pins, glass buttons, mother of pearl buckle, small shipping tag, pigment and dye inks, silk ribbon

Heritage Photographs Album
Album, walnut inked tag (7 Gypsies) label and "heritage" epoxy stickers, concho, red and burgundy ribbons (Li'l Davis Designs), crackle stamp (Stampin' Up!), "photographs" stamp (Limited Edition), postage cancellation stamp (Hero Arts), velvet leaf (ARTchix Studio), decorative nailhead (JewelCraft), silk flower, vintage fabric, lace, crochet, gauze, pigment and dye stamping inks

Inspire Romance
Printed paper (Design Originals), reproduction photograph transparency (ARTchix Studio), beaded fringe (Hobby Lobby), floss, fibers, tapestry fabric, glass slide, copper tape

You Define Love
Fabric paper (K & Company), twill (Creek Bank Creations), walnut ink (Fiber Scraps), alphabet stamps (Hero Arts), spiral paper clip (Cavallini and Co.), vintage dictionary book spine, ribbon, thread, pigment stamping inks

Flower Girls
Striped paper (DMD), metallic rub-ons (unknown), vintage girls image, floral fabric scrap, vintage buttons, birdie charm, seam binding

Wish
Printed paper, faux stone embellishment (Creative Imaginations), printable fabric (FiberMark), metal embellishment, fabric

Pages 44-45 Fusible Fiber Tags
Disneyland 1981
Epoxy word, letter and black circle stickers, panoramic photograph (Creative Imaginations), paper label holders (Club Scrap), glitter glue (Ranger), printed paper (Scrappy Cat Creations), fusible fibers (Stampendous!), inkjet photo paper (Epson), tag die-cuts (Sizzix), tickets (Limited Edition), alphabet stamps (Hero Arts), labels (Dymo), fibers, eyelets, brads, dye stamping ink

Live in My Heart
Printed transparency, reproduction photograph, ribbon (ARTchix Studio), Butterfly stamp, foam adhesive (Stampin' Up!), saying and dimensional stickers (K & Company), fusible fibers (Stampendous!), tag (American Tag Co.), dye stamping ink

Halloween Greetings
Fusible fibers (Stampendous!) reproduction child ephemera (Design Originals), cardstock (DMD), labels (Dymo), vintage popcorn ephemera, dye stamping ink, ribbon, staples

Hold Me
File folder, "E" stencil (Autumn Leaves), fusible fibers (Stampendous!), typewriter keys, "Hold Me" and butterfly transparencies (ARTchix Studio), glass microscope slide (American Science Surplus), inkjet transparency (Epson), "1939" stamp (Making Memories), black pen, ribbon, eyelets, heat set stamping inks

Asian Infusion
Fusible fibers (Stampendous!), handmade gold paper (Emagination Crafts), mulberry papers (DMD), Asian stamp (Plaid), Asian charm (Magic Scraps), bamboo clip (Anima Designs), gold paint, gold floss

Miracle
Fusible fibers (Stampendous!), beads (Blue Moon Beads), rub-on words (Making Memories), wire, thread

Pages 46-47 Glass Tags
1915 Vacation
Printed paper (Design Originals), reproduction photographs, typewriter keys (ARTchix Studio) dimensional glaze (Ranger), glass tags and corners (Stampington & Co.), shell stamps (Hero Arts), "post card" stamp (Stampin Up!), inkjet water color paper (Epson), chalk, ribbon, acrylic paint, vellum, dye stamping ink

Le Pont de Salata Constantinople
Copper tape (USArtQuest), solder (M.C. Canfield Sons), glass slide, ribbon

Remember
Shipping tag (DMD), photographic transparencies, clock stamp (Limited Edition), "Remember" epoxy sticker (Creative Imaginations), glass microscope slides (American Science Surplus), beads (Fusion Glass), floss, dye stamping ink

The Roses Have Faded
Glass microscope slide (American Science Surplus), transferred rose transparency (Limited Edition), script stamp (Hero Arts), cardstock (DMD), metal rose and leaves (ARTchix Studio), paper clip, dye stamping ink

Love Album
Album (Kolo), harlequin stencil (Delta), printed rose paper (Creative Imaginations), glass tag (Stampington & Co.), heat set stamping ink

Dichroic Illusions
Glass tag (Stampington & Co.), opalescent plastic (Cardeaux Trimmings), dimensional glaze (Plaid), wire, ribbon

Pages 48-49 Handmade Paper Tags
From Our Garden
Handmade paper kit, tag template, inclusions (Arnold Grummer), ink jet photo paper (Epson), ink jet canvas (Creative Imaginations), cardstock (DMD), velvet leaves (ARTchix Studio), labels (Dymo), spiral paper clip (Creative Impressions) red photo corners (Kolo), dye stamping inks, ribbon

Nurture Life
Handmade paper tag made with paper making kit and tag template (Arnold Grummer), cardstock (DMD), bird and "floral" reproduction ephemera (ARTchix Studio), butterfly and flower photographic stickers (Paper House Productions), flower seed packet sticker (Art Accents), harlequin stamp (Stampin' Up!), alphabet stamps (Hero Arts), glitter glue (Ranger), colored hemp cord (Beadery), index tab (Z-International), plastic flower, eyelet, dye stamping ink

He Loves Me He Loves Me Not
Handmade papers (Provo Craft), paper flower (Making Memories), reproduction photograph (ARTchix Studio), silk tassels (Hot Off The Press), decorative eyelet (Creative Imaginations), decorative nailhead (JewelCraft), tag die-cut (Sizzix), dye stamping ink

Grandmother
Handmade papers (Provo Craft), fusible fibers (Stampendous!), dried flowers (Pressed Petals), swirl stamp (Postmodern Design), tiny glass marbles (Magic Scraps), gold metal frame and charm (JewelCraft), micro beads (Magic Scraps), gold paint, gold floss, fiber

Life is Good
Handmade paper, tassel (Provo Craft), paper flowers (Making Memories) wire butterfly (Westrim), charms (JewelCraft), ribbon, brads

Stick Your Neck Out!
Handmade mesh paper (Gami Goods), "Adventure" printed twill (Creative Impressions), cardstock (DMD), leopard velour paper, copper charm (unknown), ribbon

Pages 50-51 Mat Board Tags
Hunter 5 Years Old
Cardstock (DMD, Paper Adventures), mat board (Hobby Lobby), alphabet stamps (Hero Arts, Stamp Craft), circle stamps (Paper Candy), labels (Dymo), typewriter keys (ARTchix Studio), eyelets, ribbon, dye stamping inks, handmade letter "H" stencil

The Real West
Die-cut mat board (K & Company), "Cowboy", "Yee-Haw", star stickers, printed leather and canvas papers (Creative Imaginations), blue printed paper (Scrappy Cat Creations), twine (Magic Scraps), cowboy and calf images, cut out words, vintage metal stamp, dye stamping inks

Smile
Mat board, printed artist tape (Club Scrap), crackle printed paper (Me & My Big Ideas), "Smile" sticker (Pebbles), rose sticker (Paper House Productions) crackle modeling paste (USArtQuest), walnut ink (Anima Designs), glitter glue (Ranger), ribbon, eyelet

Soul Paintings
Label holders, epoxy letter and saying stickers, rub-on date (Creative Imaginations), photo tinting oils (Marshall's), frame cut-out (Sizzix), vintage paint-by-numbers on mat board, ribbon, fibers, brads

Child of Adoption Easel Frame
Die-cut mat board frame, ticket stamp (Club Scrap), green rub-on letters, lime glitter paper, decorative eyelet (Creative Imaginations), iridescent acrylic paint (Golden Artist Colors), cardstock (DMD), embossed paper (Paper Adventures), ink jet photo paper (Epson), "Cherish" sticker, date stamp (Making Memories), glitter glue (Ranger), ribbon, brads, black pen, stamping ink saying cut from vintage book

Crow
Printed paper, rooster sticker (Karen Foster Design), gesso (Golden Artist Colors), table cloth stamp (JudiKins), textured green cardstock (Bazzill), canvas letters (Li'l Davis Designs), mini colored safety pins (Making Memories), mini suspender clip (Prym-Dritz), chicken wire, cardboard, dye stamping ink

Pages 52-53 Mesh Tags
Love, Live and Learn Thru Your Garden
Album (DMD), printed paper, mesh, faux wax seals, "learn" epoxy sticker, decorative eyelets (Creative Imaginations), dye stamping inks, glitter glue (Ranger), inkjet photo paper (Epson), labels (Dymo), date Stamp (Making Memories), words cut from vintage book, ribbon

Girlfriend Album
Album (Mrs. Grossman's), tag base (Club Scrap), woven label (Me & My Big Ideas), copper mesh (AMACO), flower punch (Emagination Crafts), rhinestone brads (Magic Scraps), dye stamping ink, vintage fabric, ribbon

Crazy M
Metal mesh, "M" charm (Making Memories), printed paper (Anna Griffin), printed epoxy sticker (Creative Imaginations), word label sticker (Pebbles), definition (Foofala), brads, ribbon, black cardstock, staples

Kennedy
Printed paper (Design Originals), mesh (AMACO), tag (unknown), brads, fabric, jute

Maddy
Printed paper and transparency, star stickers (Creative Imaginations), colored staples (Making Memories), alphabet stamps (Hero Arts), jute, jute mesh, ribbon, leather

Copper Leaf
Copper bookplates (Li'l Davis Designs), copper charms (Foofala), mesh (Magic Mesh), skeleton leaf (unknown), copper brads, ribbon

Pages 54-55 Mica Tags
Summer Fishing
Album (Autumn Leaves), printed papers (Design Originals), mica (USArtQuest), ink jet photo paper (Epson), velvet leaves (ARTchix Studio), decorative eyelets (Creative Imaginations), spiral paper clip (Cavallini and Co.), mini brads (Karen Foster Design), label holder (unknown), acrylic paint, fibers

Art and Soul
Tag (7 Gypsies), mica (USArtQuest), epoxy and postage stamp stickers, "Art" rub-on letters (Creative Imaginations), decorative stamp (Making Memories), alphabet stamp (PSX Design), bottle cap, negative strip

Spiritual
Tag (7 Gypsies), mica (USArtQuest), printed paper (Creative Imaginations), alphabet stamps (PSX Design), staple, Asian charm, lace

Smile
Mica (USArtQuest), jump rings (Westrim), textured paper (FiberMark), alphabet stamps (PSX Design), leather cord, mini tags, bingo card

Fifties Foods
Mica (USArtQuest), alphabet stamps (Ma Vinci's Reliquary), rub-on letters (Creative Imaginations), scalloped metal tape (Hobby Lobby), black extra thick embossing powder, glitter, eyelets, ribbon, solvent stamping ink, vintage food images

Southwestern Tag
Mica (USArtQuest), beads (Cousins Corporation), hand clip (Westrim), lizard stamps (Stamp A Mania), copper embossing powder, feathers, wire, embossing stamping ink

Pages 56-57 Modern Ephemera Tags
Thrift Store Shopping
Printed paper (K & Company), cardstocks (Club Scrap), ink jet photo paper (Epson), file folder (Autumn Leaves), mini alphabet stamps (Hero Arts), glitter glue (Ranger), date stamp (unknown), vintage blue and white fabric, green rickrack, thread, price tags, acrylic paint, ribbon, dye stamping ink

He Drinks a Latte
Cup and alphabet stamps (Club Scrap), labels (Dymo), mini instant film (Polaroid), staples, cup, corrugated paper, fibers, paper clip, pigment and stamping inks

Looking for a Car
Tag (American Tag Co.), colored hemp cord (Beadery), lowercase alphabet stamps (Hero Arts), uppercase alphabet stamps (Plaid), cardstock (DMD), car charm (Boutique Trims), newspaper, image of eyes, dye stamping ink

Breakfast (6:00) at Tiffany's
Black artist's tape (Graphic Arts), spoon cut-out (DMD), Audrey "sticker" (US Post Office), vintage postcard scrap, bias tape, seam binding

Lantern Party
Reproduction photograph (ARTchix Studio), lantern stickers (Gifted Line), beads (unknown), die-cut business card holder tag, ribbon, floss

Going Crazy
"Crazy" alphabet stamps, acrylic paint (Making Memories), "Going" alphabet stamps (Plaid), rub-on letters (Creative Imaginations), airline tickets

Pages 58-59 Negative Tags
New York Exposed
Printed and plain cardstock, printed vellum, printed tape, fibers (Club Scrap), Negative strips, white rub-on letters (Creative Imaginations), ink jet photo paper (Epson), Label holder and "tag art" stamps (Limited Edition), alphabet stamps (Ma Vinci's Reliquary), nailheads (JewelCraft), photo corners (Kolo), labels (Dymo), staples, stamping inks, negative strips

Discover Nature
Negative transparency (Creative Imaginations), photographic die-cut butterfly and flower (Paper House Productions), butterfly postage (Li'l Davis Designs), spiral clip (Creative Impressions), "Discover" sticker (Pebbles), undeveloped film, staples

Cherish, Faith and Inspire
Rose stickers (Paper House Productions), mesh (Magenta), eyelet stickers (Stampendous!), woven labels (Me & My Big Ideas), fibers, negative strips

You Are My Sunshine
Collage paper (DMD), blue printed paper (Deluxe Designs), blue and white mini circle punched stickers (Scrappy Cat Creations), ribbon

Where There Is Love
Metal-rimmed heart tag, negative transparency (Creative Imaginations), cork (Creative Impressions), quote sticker (Karen Foster Design), printed filmstrip tissue paper (DMD), glitter glue (Ranger), alphabet stamps (La Pluma), mesh (Gami Goods), red tiny glass marbles (Deco Arts), decorative paper embellishments (Me & My Big Ideas), red beaded ribbon (unknown), negative pieces, ribbon, ticket, "Reunion" license plate, bottle cap

Pretty in Pink
Handmade paper (Artistic Scrapper), flower bouquet from printed paper (Design Originals), decorative paper clip (EK Success), square "P" clip (Scrapworks), rectangle fastener (7 Gypsies), pigment stamping ink, fabric, embossing powder

Pages 60-61 Page Protector Tags
Sinatra Likes...
Printed paper, letter stickers, starburst charm, decorative eyelets (Creative Imaginations), page protectors (Mrs. Grossman's), leopard rolling stamp (Clearsnap), boomerang stamp (Paper Candy), mini alphabet stamps (Hero Arts), ink jet photo paper (Epson), spiral paper clip (Cavallini and Co.), metal colorant (Ranger), cat food, toy, catnip, ribbon, fiber, dye stamping ink

Florida Sunrise
Page protector (Mrs. Grossman's), decorative eyelet (Creative Imaginations), labels (Dymo), dye stamping ink, vintage gauze fabric, seashells

Thank You Card
Printed papers (Me & My Big Ideas), typewriter stamps, circle metal-rimmed tag (EK Success), bookplate stamp (Rubber Stampede), card (Hero Arts), page protector (Mrs. Grossman's), nailhead (JewelCraft), ribbon, dye stamping ink, marker, rose petals

Birthday Greetings
Page protector (Mrs. Grossman's), plastic raffia (Paper Adventures), star brad (Creative Imaginations), printed paper hole reinforcement (Design Originals), confetti, vintage postcard, thread

Art, Spirit, Inspire
Page protector (Mrs. Grossman's), printed paper (NRN Designs), tag die-cut (Sizzix), rub-on words (Creative Imaginations), printed hole reinforcement (EK Success), alcohol inks (USArtQuest), ribbon, painter's tape, vellum

Keep Your Face to the Sunshine
Fabric corners, transparency quote (Making Memories), butterfly sticker (Paper House Productions), snap (Doodlebug Design), metal flower charm (American Traditional Designs), butterfly charm (Boxer Scrapbook Productions), acrylic sun (Heidi Grace Designs), rose stamp (All Night Media), yellow printed paper (Scrappy Cat Creations), ribbon, buttons, solvent ink

Pages 62-63 Paper Photo Frame Tags
Friends
Floral printed paper (Li'l Davis Designs), measuring tape printed paper (K & Company), cardstock (DMD), mini paper photo frames, paper tag topers (Heart and Home Collectables Inc.), script, mini alphabet stamps (Hero Arts), calligraphy stencil (Wordsworth), glitter glue (Ranger), decorative eyelet, letter stickers (Creative Imaginations), labels (Dymo), inkjet photo paper (Epson), date stamp (unknown), eyelets, ribbon, vintage paper frame, belt buckle, dye stamping ink, acrylic paint

Treasure
Reproduction paper frame (Melissa Frances), circle, dot stamps (Hero Arts), glitter glue, (Ranger), "Treasure" epoxy sticker (Creative Imaginations), ribbon, pigment stamping inks

A Rose-Colored World
Printed oval frame (Anna Griffin), reproduction photograph, velvet leaves (ARTchix Studio), glitter glue (Ranger), vintage buttons

Altered Photo Frame
Reproduction paper frame (Melissa Frances/ Heart & Home), printed paper (Design Originals), decorative tape (Grafix), dimensional glaze (Plaid), reproduction photograph (ARTchix Studio) thread

Sierra and Gina
Red crochet cotton, star charms (ARTchix Studio), tag with window (DMD), colored staples (Making Memories), stencils (unknown), paint, confetti, handmade soda can charms with eyelets

My Heart Flutters
Reproduction paper frame (Melissa Frances/ Heart & Home), metal-rimmed heart tag (Creative Imaginations), crackle stamp (Stampendous!), spiral stamp (Stamp a Mania), text and woman image (DMD), metal dots (Scrap Arts), fasteners (Colorbök); ribbon, chalk

Pages 64-65 Pet Identification Tags
Courage
Blue and red printed papers (Wordsworth), golden printed paper (K & Company), ink jet watercolor paper (Epson), letter and patriot stickers (Sticker Studio), ephemera transparencies (ARTchix Studio), star nailheads (JewelCraft), crackle stamp (Stamping Up!), texture stamp (Club Scrap), labels (Dymo), "Courage" heart pet identification tag (Quick Tag), ribbon, pigment stamping ink, acrylic paint

Heritage Photo Box
Photo box (Kolo), metal dog tag (American Tag Co.), steel alphabet stamps (Harbor Freight Tools), metallic rub-ons (Craf-T), printed paper (Creative Imaginations), labels (Dymo)

Travel Album
Handmade album kit and binding discs (Rollabind), reproduction postcard and plane photograph (Me & My Big Ideas), postage stamps (Toybox), pet identification tags, travel rubber stamps (Club Scrap), "Travel" alphabet stamps (Hero Arts), printed epoxy hole reinforcement (EK Success), eyelet, ribbon, solvent and pigment inks

Her Tender Heart
Pet identification (Club Scrap), tag die-cut (Sizzix), ink jet photo canvas (Creative Imaginations), gold rub-on words and graphics (Autumn Leaves), rhinestone brad (Magic Scraps), rhinestones, vintage paint-by-numbers, fabric embellishment

Adore
"Adore" heart pet identification tag (Quick Tag), beads (JewelCraft), walnut ink (Fiber Scraps), round epoxy sticker (Creative Imaginations), printed die-cut (Paper House Productions) line stamp (Magenta), vintage coin tubes, loose leaf paper ring, rhinestones, thread

Dog Tags
Paper and metal tags (Magic Scraps), "C" chain (Scrapyard 329), ball chain (Westrim), circle metal letter stencils (Scrapworks), dog charms (JewelCraft), vintage dog ephemera

Pages 66-67 Photographic Tags
Smile, Giggle, Play
Cardstock (DMD), printed paper (KI Memories), mesh sheet (Magenta), glitter glue (Ranger), metal words (Making Memories), spiral paper clips (Cavallini and Co.), label maker (Dymo), vellum, dye stamping ink, ribbon, acrylic paint, words cut from vintage book, thread

Sunshine
Inkjet transparency (Epson), stripe printed paper (KI Memories), "Sunshine" sticker (Stampendous!), orange vellum, ribbon, handmade tag, gear

Denver 1993
Rub-on words and numbers, brad (Creative Imaginations), picture hanger, ribbon, handmade tag

Digital Beauty
"Beauty" Asian rubber stamps (Anima Designs), photo paper (Kodak), transparency- printed photo, handmade tag, scanned leaves

Effusion
Printed paper (Li'l Davis Designs), silver frame (Scrapworks), definition (Foofala), black cardstock, staples

Imagine, Achieve, Embrace
Wire words, cardstock (Pixie Press), ball chain (Making Memories), metal tape (USArtQuest), alphabet stamps (PSX Design), solvent stamping ink, fibers, paint swatches

Pages 68-69 Plastic Tags
Kiss, Smooch, Pucker Up
Mosaic printed paper (Paper Adventures), printed paper (KI Memories), Watercolor printed paper (Wordsworth), mesh (Magenta), scribble paper (Handmade) Plastic tags (Heidi Grace Designs), letter sticker "templates" brad rub-ons, "Pucker up" sticker (Creative Imaginations), mosaic stamp (Stampendous!), lip stamp (Rubber Stampede), alphabet stamps (Ma Vinci's Reliquary), labels (Dymo), ticket punch (EK Success), photo corners (Kolo), inkjet photo paper (Epson), brads, dye stamping inks, embossing powder

School Days Album
Album (Mrs. Grossman's), printed paper, letter stickers, (Li'l Davis Designs), plastic ruler, ribbon

Play
Plastic playing cards (Kikkerland), wood letters (Li'l Davis Designs), copper paint pen (Krylon), mini dominos, puzzle piece, brad, eyelet, solvent stamping ink

Oh Friend O' My Life
Faux leopard fur (Grafix), slide mounts (DMD), butterfly sticker (Paper House Productions), glass flowers (House of Marbles), beads (Beadery, Halcraft, Westrim), printed transparency (Memories Complete)

Treasure
Printed papers (DMD, 4 Altered Minds), charms (The Card Connection), decorative eyelet (Creative Imaginations), rub-on words (Making Memories), buttons, ribbon, vintage doily

Honey-Do
Plastic tags, stamps (Sunday Intl.), glitter (Stampendous!), corrugated paper (DMD), gold paint pen (Krylon), embossed paper (Provo Craft), metal flowers (JewelCraft), dimensional glaze (Plaid), colored pens, ribbon, embossing powder

Pages 70-71 Polymer Clay Tags
Lexington Cemetery
Stone and Crackle printed cardstock (Club Scrap), text paper (K & Company), Inkjet photo and transparency papers (Epson), polymer clay, push mold (Polyform Products), micaceous iron oxide acrylic paint (Golden Artist Colors), medallion stamps (Stampendous!), stone etching stamp (Hero Arts), circle-rimmed tags (American Tag Co.), ink jet photo paper (Epson), statue transparencies (ARTchix Studio), vintage ribbon, stamping inks

Polymer Hanging Tag
Polymer clay, templates (Polyform Products), iridescent pigment powders (Ranger), rubber stamps (Hampton Arts, Inkadinkado, Limited Edition, Postmodern Designs), ribbon, pigment stamping ink, acrylic paint

Voyage
Tag (7 Gypsies), printed papers (K & Company), letter stickers (Creative Imaginations), polymer clay (Polyform Products), metallic pigment powders (USArtQuest), alphabet stamps, mesh fabric, clip

Home Sweet Home
Polymer clay (Polyform Products), handmade paper (Provo Craft), patterned paper (Design Originals), "Home Sweet Home" sticker (Karen Foster Design), keyhole charm (Li'l Davis Designs), printed twill (unknown), pigment and embossing inks

Dream, Hope, Wonder
Polymer clay (Polyform Products), printed paper (Anna Griffin), rub-on words (Making Memories), hole reinforcement (Cloud 9 Design), fibers

Pages 72-73 Ribbon Tags
Couture 1968
Dress pattern printed paper, number epoxy stickers, circle metal frames (Li'l Davis Designs), printed papers (KI Memories), ink jet photo paper (Epson), photographic rose die-cuts (Paper House Productions), calligraphy ink (Salis International), alphabet stamps (Club Scrap), acrylic paint, buttons, vintage clothing labels, various ribbons, belt, dye stamping ink

She's Happy
Reproduction photograph (ARTchix Studio), tag die-cut (Sizzix), glitter glue (Ranger), decorative hole reinforcement (EK Success), words cut from vintage magazine, ribbon

My Love
Alphabet stamps (PSX Design), printed paper, bag (unknown), ribbon, heart, eyelet, envelope

Madeline
Textured paper (FiberMark), brads, ribbon, fabric

Jenn B.
Decorative brad, ball chain, word charm, eyelet letter, definition sticker, rub-on words (Making Memories), printed papers (Li'l Davis Designs), striped printed paper, perforated letters (Mustard Moon), fabric paper (K & Company), ephemera (Me & My Big Ideas), wire treble clef (EK Success), ribbon, jump rings, staples, glassine envelope

Mom
Patterned paper, key embellishment (Li'l Davis Designs), metal frame (K & Company), "Mom" buttons (MOD), ribbon

Pages 74-75 Shaped Metal-Rimmed Tags
Mother and Daughter
Printed paper, shaped metal-rimmed tags, faux wax seal, epoxy stickers, letter and border stickers, rub-on letters (Creative Imaginations), cardstock (DMD), glitter glue (Ranger), word plaque stamps (Limited Edition), script stamp (Hero Arts), date stamp (unknown), inkjet photo paper (Epson), photo corners (K & Company), ribbon, brad, dye stamping ink

Amour, Amour!
Wood triptych (Walnut Hallow), printed papers, stamp letter stickers, heart metal-rimmed tag (Creative Imaginations), reproduction transparency photo, velvet leaves (ARTchix Studio), nailheads, bead (JewelCraft), silk flower (Michaels), straight pin, ribbon, stamping ink

Heaven Sent
Frame, crackle patterned paper, woven label (Me & My Big Ideas), copper paint pen (Ranger), reproduction photograph (ARTchix Studio), copper tape (USArtQuest), shipping tag (American Tag Co.), mini tag (DMD), script stamp (Hero Arts), flower transparency (Magic Scraps), watercolor ink jet photo paper (Epson), eyelets, ribbon, pigment stamping ink

Flower Bouquet
Flower metal-rimmed tags (Creative Imaginations), photographic flower die-cuts (Paper House Productions), velvet leaves (ARTchix Studio)

Boulder, CO 1993
Reproduction postcard, postage stamp sticker, trim (Me & My Big Ideas), "Photographs" stamp (Limited Edition), copper tape (USArtQuest), tag die-cut (Sizzix), cyanotype paper (Nature Print Paper), dye stamping ink, pen

Tasha
Shaped metal-rimmed tag, ink jet canvas paper (Creative Imaginations), label (Dymo), cardstock (DMD), dye stamping ink, ribbon

Pages 76-77 Shrink Plastic Tags
Travel in New Orleans
Album (7 Gypsies), shrink plastic sheets, small die-cut tags, border stamp (Stampendous!), large die-cut shrink plastic tags (Sizzix), photo tag template (Creative Memories), alphabet stamps (Ma Vinci's Reliquary), mini alphabet stamps, script stamps (Hero Arts), clock stamp (Limited Edition), postage stamp (Club Scrap), circle metal-rimmed tag (EK Success), corner and hole reinforcement stickers (Sticker Studio), copper fibers (Inkadinkado), ribbon, dye and heat set stamping inks

Wish Upon a Star
Cardstocks (DMD), interference acrylic paint (Golden Artist Colors), star printed paper (Reminiscence Paper), clear die-cut shrink plastic sun, gold paint pen (Ranger), reproduction photograph (ARTchix Studio), tag die-cut (Sizzix), "Wish" epoxy sticker (Creative Imaginations), printed epoxy hole reinforcement (EK Success), gold thread, fibers

She's So Nutty
Hole reinforcement stickers, black shrink plastic tags (Stampendous!), handbag, gloves and purse stamps (Hero Arts), printed stripe paper (KI Memories), vintage magazine images and words, glitter glue (Ranger), charms (Westrim), ribbon, fibers, paint chip

Her Jewel-Tone Heart
Black shrink plastic sheet, texture stamp (Stampendous!), reproduction photograph, circle punch (Emagination Crafts), iridescent acrylic paint (Golden Artist Colors), copper wire (JewelCraft), "Heart" epoxy sticker (Creative Imaginations), vintage button and card

Memories
Clear shrink plastic sheet (Stampendous!), alcohol inks (USArtQuest), rubber stamps (Hampton Arts, Rubber Stampede), alphabet stamps (Plaid), postage stamp sticker (Me & My Big Ideas), metal frame (K & Company), reproduction photograph (DMD), clock hand (Hot Off The Press), label letter stickers (Pebbles), vintage dictionary page, ribbon, solvent ink

Go With Your Heart
Background and initial stamp (Anna Griffin), decorative stamp (Stampability), shrink plastic (Shrinky Dink), silver and clear embossing powders, embossing and pigment stamping inks

Pages 78-79 Slide Mount Tags
Tacky State Plate Collection
Printed papers and slide mounts (Design Originals), plastic slide mounts (Loersch), typewriter keys (ARTchix Studio), label and "Welcome to" stickers (Pebbles), large alphabet stamps (Ma Vinci's Reliquary), small alphabet stamps (Hero Arts), inkjet photo papers (Epson), laminate for photo transfer (Therm O Web), mini tag (DMD), library pocket and card (Limited Edition), eyelets, ribbon, fibers, pigment stamping inks

Miss. Ferne 1920's
Slide mount, printed paper (Design Originals), laminate (Therm O Web), pressed pansies, ground mica (USArtQuest), ink jet transparency (Epson), heart charm (Boutique Trims), rub-on letter (Creative Imaginations), picture hardware, ribbon, brad

Doc and Gert Laugh
Printed hole reinforcement (EK Success), dimensional glaze (JudiKins), scripts stamp (unknown), paint chip, vintage key, dye stamping ink, ribbon, slide mount, brads

Indy
Mini circle rimmed tags, letter stickers, bone punch (EK Success), leather paper (K & Company), tag die-cut (Sizzix), slide mounts (Loersch), pewter dog accent (Magenta), ball chain (Westrim), dog clip (Karen Foster Design), ribbon, rhinestones

Glamour Girl
Black printed papers (DMD), printed papers (Colorbök), metal tags (Magic Scraps), face stamp (Hampton Arts), women stamps (Hero Arts), reproduction photograph (ARTchix Studio), beaded trim (Hirschberg Shutz and Company), large eyelet (Prym-Dritz), silver paint pen, solvent ink, ribbon

Boyhood
Paper slide mounts, file folder (DMD), decorative eyelet (Creative Imaginations), decorative paperclips (EK Success), wood letters (Li'l Davis Designs), printed paper (Design Originals), stamps (Hero Arts), fibers, pigment stamping ink

Pages 80-81 Sticker Tags
The Beauty of a Single Flower
Printed papers, tag, letter, postage stamp, architectural stickers, wire word, faux wax seal, (Creative Imaginations), letter stamps (Stamp Craft), date stamp (Making Memories), ribbon, brads, dye and spray inks, embossing powder, vintage book page, square punch

Adore
Printed papers, printed epoxy, square, border, saying and letter stickers (Creative Imaginations), reproduction photograph (ARTchix Studio), glitter glue (Ranger), silver buckle (Jest Charming), vintage ribbon, purple cardstock, fibers, pigment stamping inks

Eclectic
Tag (7 Gypsies), printed vellum, postage stamp letter stickers (Creative Imaginations), reproduction ephemera (Foofala), postage stamps, iridescent medium (unknown), fabric

Accomplishment, Appreciation, Perseverance
Word stickers (Club Scrap), rose stickers (K & Company), white twill (Creek Bank Creations), ribbon charm (Making Memories), tags (unknown), green cardstock, fibers

Journey
Printed papers (DMD, Rusty Pickle), collage elements (Limited Edition), postage rubber stamps (Inkadinkado), ball chain, "travel" sticker, rub-on words (Making Memories), vintage book page

Family Game Night
Game printed paper, transparency, slide mount (Design Originals), "Game" alphabet stickers (Me & My Big Ideas), typewriter letter stickers (K & Company), epoxy letter stickers (K & Company), decorative eyelet (Creative Imaginations), fibers, ribbon

Pages 82-83 Transparency Tags
Poipu Beach
Printed transparency tag, faux wax seal, teal printed paper (Creative Imaginations), Ocean printed transparency (Magic Scraps), shipping tags, copper brads (American Tag Co.), alphabet stamps (Ma Vinci's Reliquary), swirl stamp, cardstock (Club Scrap), vellum letter stickers (Mrs. Grossman's), postage stamps (Art Accents), number stickers (Sticker Studio), metal label holder (Li'l Davis Designs), photo corners (Canson), ink jet photo paper (Epson), mini tag (DMD), mini alphabet stamps (Hero Arts), fibers, pigment stamping inks, book, negative strip, tissue paper

Blue
Blue printed transparency (ARTchix Studio), silver clips (7 Gypsies), decorative eyelet (Creative Imaginations), alphabet stamps (Ma Vinci's Reliquary), solvent stamping ink, negative strips, fibers, acrylic paints

Twenty Carat
Printed transparency (Magic Scraps), tan printed paper (Me & My Big Ideas), label holder (Li'l Davis Designs), tag template, printed hole reinforcement (EK Success), vintage image, black and white words, paint chip, fibers, buttons

Game of Life
Printed paper (Design Originals), decorative paper clips (EK Success), printed transparencies (ARTchix Studio), copper paint pen (Ranger), tag die-cut (Sizzix), wire thread

Mystery
Printed transparency (Magic Scraps), textured paper (FiberMark), word label sticker (Pebbles), definition (Foofala), bingo card, clips, fabric

1953
Linen paper (FiberMark), printed transparency (Creative Imaginations), number stickers (Pebbles), mini tag, star stamp, safety pin, clips, staples

Pages 84-85 Ultra Thick Embossing Powder Tags
Laugh
Printed paper, "K" and "N" index cards and rub-on letters, "V" letter stencil (Autumn Leaves), negative strip, "Laugh" wire word, label holder, "A" bottle cap sticker, decorative eyelet (Creative Imaginations), mini file folder, shipping tags (DMD), black, pearl and clear extra thick embossing powder (Ranger), alphabet stamps, "K" and "V" letter stencils (Ma Vinci's Reliquary), ticket, vintage labels, numbers stamp (Limited Edition), nailheads (JewelCraft), circle metal-rimmed tag, square shipping tag (American Tag Co.), inkjet photo paper (Epson) text stamp (Hero Arts), circle line art stamp (Paper Candy), hand stamp (Toybox), bingo card with script stamp (Stampers Anonymous), labels (Dymo), printed rubber band (7 Gypsies), spiral paper clip (unknown), brads, staples, ribbon, fibers, colored pencils, vintage bingo card, acrylic paint, handmade mini dot stamp, black pen, corner punch, embossing powder, stamping ink, eyelets

Kirk and Roo
Chipboard tag, cardstock (DMD), black extra thick embossing powder (Ranger), ribbon, wood letters (Li'l Davis Designs), inkjet photo paper (Epson), label (Dymo), staples, dye and embossing stamping inks

Imagine
Ink jet photo paper (Epson), photographic butterfly die-cut (Paper House Productions) Clear extra thick embossing powder (Ranger), glitter (Magic Scraps), metal word (Li'l Davis Designs), die-cut tag (Sizzix), ribbon, fibers

Just Married
Chipboard tag, reproduction photograph (DMD), clear extra thick embossing powder (Ranger), pressed pansies, "opal" chips (USArtQuest), charms (Boutique Trims), fibers, embossing powder

In This Joyful and Happy Hour...
Slide mount (DMD), extra thick embossing powder (Ranger), fabric, clips, cardstock, lace, ephemera

Observation
Stamps (Stampers Anonymous), extra thick embossing powder (Ranger), tags (unknown), dye stamping inks, fibers

Pages 86-87 Vintage Ephemera Tags
Pam's Baby Shower
Paint crackle and grey mottled papers (Me & My Big Ideas), printed transparency (Magic Scraps), cardstock (DMD), ink jet photo paper (Epson), mesh (I Love Scrapbooking), labels (Dymo), ticket (Limited Edition), ribbon, eyelet, pigment stamping inks, handmade foam stamp and printed photo mat, photo corner punch, vintage baby image, book page, thread

So Perfect
Reproduction ephemera, woven label (Me & My Big Ideas), die-cut tag (Sizzix), ink jet photo paper (Epson), glitter glue (Ranger), star brad (Creative Imaginations), soda pop tab

Camera Shy
Printed hole reinforcements (EK Success), reproduction photograph on ink jet transparency (unknown), vintage tag ticket and words cut from book

Tally
Dimensional glaze (JudiKins), vintage bridge tally card, photographs, domino ribbon, red rhinestones

Cool Fridges
File folder, printed paper (DMD), labels (Dymo), ball chain (Boxer), vintage fridge ads, gingham ribbon, corner rounder

French Fashion
Black trim (Me & My Big Ideas)
Paris, Milano and style post stamps (Hero Arts), fleur de lis charm (Nunn Designs) mini circle-rimmed tags, letter stickers, dress, tiara, glove stickers (EK Success), walnut ink (7 Gypsies, Fiber Scraps), Eiffel tower (Silver Crow), reproduction photograph (ARTchix Studio), gold glitter glue (Duncan), colored pencils, solvent stamping ink, pigment stamping ink, button, vintage watch, large tag, yellow rose, bow, hat pin, fabric, lace

Pages 88-89 Wood Tags
Bloom and Grow
Plant printed paper, pressed flower, saying stickers, faux stone embellishments (Creative Imaginations), wood tags (Limited Edition, Fosters), mica flakes (USArtQuest), tie-dye printed paper (Club Scrap), dye stamping inks (Ranger), walnut ink (Anima Designs), ink jet photo paper (Epson), brush marker (EK Success), thread, pressed flowers

Their Good Bye
Wood craft sticks (The Chenille Kraft Company), printed papers (KI Memories), glitter glue (Ranger), ball chain (Westrim), hear punch, vintage images and words

Parrot Brand Oranges
Wood veneer tag (American Tag Co.), cardstock (DMD), fruit crate sticker (Art Accents), ribbon, acrylic paint, brads

Luca
Wood veneer sheets (Emagination Crafts), wood letters (Li'l Davis Designs), pewter hand charm (Making Memories), printed slide mount (Design Originals), metallic rub-ons (Craf-T), mesh (Magic Mesh), blender pen (ChartPak)

Gold Kissed Foliage
Wood tag (Laura's Craft), gold paint pen (Krylon), embossing powder, embossing ink, acrylic paint, wire, fibers

Discover the Journey
Wood tag (Laura's Craft), stencil (Scrapworks), letter stickers (Pebbles), fibers, twigs (7 Gypsies), raffia, hemp twine, handmade paper

SOURCES

The following companies manufacture products showcased throughout this book. I would like to thank them for their contributions and support, which has made the art featured in this book possible.

3L Corp.
(800) 828-3130
www.scrapbook-adhesives.com

3M
(800) 364-3577
www.3m.com

7 Gypsies
(800) 588-6707
www.7gypsies.com

All Night Media
(see Plaid Enterprises)

American Art Clay Co. (AMACO)
(800) 374-1600
www.amaco.com

American Crafts
(801) 2226-0747
www.americancrafts.com

American Tag Co.
(800) 223-3956
www.americantag.net

Anima Designs
(800) 570-6847
www.animadesigns.com

Anna Griffin, Inc.
(wholesale only)
(888) 817-8170
www.annagriffin.com

ARTchix Studio
(250) 370-9985
www.artchixstudio.com

Autumn Leaves (wholesale only)
(800) 588-6707
www.autumnleaves.com

Biblical Impressions
(877) 587-0941
www.biblical.com

Big Time Products, LLC (Un-du®)
(888) Buy-undu
www.un-du.com

Blue Moon Beads
(800) 377-6715
www.bluemoonbeads.com

Boutique Trims, Inc.
(248) 437-2017
www.boutiquetrims.com

Canson®, Inc.
(800) 628-9283
www.canson-us.com

Carolee's Creations®
(435) 563-1100
www.ccpaper.com

Chatterbox, Inc.
(208) 939-9133
www.chatterboxinc.com

Clearsnap, Inc.
(360) 293-6634
www.clearsnap.com

Club Scrap™, Inc.
(888) 634-9100
www.clubscrap.com

Craf-T Products
(507) 235-3996
www.craf-tproducts.com

Creative Imaginations
(800) 942-6487
www.cigift.com

Creative Impressions Rubber
Stamps, Inc.
(719) 596-4860
www.creativeimpressions.com

C-Thru® Ruler Company, The
Wholesale only)
(800) 243-8419
www.cthruruler.com

DecoArt™, Inc.
(800) 367-3047
www.decoart.com

Delta Technical Coatings, Inc.
(800) 423-4135
www.deltacrafts.com

Deluxe Designs
(480) 205-9210
www.deluxedesigns.com

Design Originals
(800) 877-0067
www.d-originals.com

DMD Industries, Inc.
(Wholesale only)
(800) 805-9890
www.dmdind.com

Doodlebug Design™ Inc.
(801) 966-9952
www.doodlebugdesinginc.com

Dr. Ph. Martin's-a division of Salis
International, Inc.
(800) 843-8293
www.docmartins.com

Duncan Enterprises
(800) 782-6748
www.duncan-enterprises .com

EK Success™, Ltd.
(Wholesale only)
(800) 524-1349
www.eksuccess.com

Ellison® Craft & Design
(800) 253-2238
www.ellison.com

Emagination Crafts, Inc.
(Wholesale only)
(630) 833-9521
www.emaginationcrafts.com

Epson America, Inc.
www.epson.com

Fiber Scraps™
(215) 230-4905
www.fiberscraps.com

Fiskars, Inc. (Wholesale only)
(715) 842-2091
www.fiskars.com

FoofaLa
(402) 758-0863
www.foofala.com

Glue Dots® International
(Wholesale only)
(888) 688-7131
www.gluedots.com

Golden Artist Colors, Inc.
(800) 959-6543
www.goldenpaints.com

Great Balls of Fiber
303-697-5942
www.greatballsoffiber.com

Heart & Home, Inc./Melissa
Frances
(905)-686-9031
www.melissafrancess.com

Heidi Grace Designs
(866) 894-3434
www.heidigrace.com

Hero Arts® Rubber Stamps, Inc.
(800) 822-4376
www.heroarts.com

Hot Off The Press, Inc.
(800) 227-9595
www.paperpizazz.com

Hot Potatoes
(615) 296-8002
www.hotpotatoes.com

Inkadinakdo® Rubber Stamps
(800) 888-4652
www.inkadinkado.com

JewelCraft LLC
(201) 223-0804
www.jewelcraft.biz

K & Company
(888) 244-2083
www.kandcompany.com

Karen Foster Design
(Wholesale only)
(801) 451-9779
www.karenfosterdesign.com

KI Memories
(972) 243-5595
www.kimemories.com

Kolo®, LLC
(888) 636-5656
www.kolo-usa.com

Krylon
(216) 566-200
www.krylon.com

Li'l Davis Designs
(949) 838-0344
www.lildavisdesigns.com

Limited Edition Rubberstamps
(650) 594-4242
www.limitededitionrs.com

Loersch Corporation USA
(610) 264-5641
www.loersch.com

Ma Vinci's Reliquary
http://crafts.dm.net/
mall/reliquary

Magenta Rubber Stamps
(Wholesale only)
(800) 565-5254
www.magentastyle.com

Magic Mesh
(615) 345-6374
www.magicmesh.com

Magic Scraps™
(972) 238-1838
www.magicscraps.com

Making Memories
(800) 286-5263
www.makingmemories.com

Marshall Company, The
(800) 621-5488
www.bkaphoto.com

May Arts
www.mayarts.com

me & my BIG ideas®
(wholesale only)
(949) 883-2065
www.meandmybigideas.com

Memories Complete™, LLC
(866) 966-6365
www.memoriescomplete.com

Mrs. Grossman's Paper
Company (Wholesale only)
(800) 429-4549
www.mrsgrossmans.com

Mustard Moon™
(408) 299-8542
www.mustardmoon.com

Nature Print Paper Products, Inc.
(925) 377-0755
www.natureprintpaper.com

NRN Designs
(800) 421-6958
www.nrndesigns.com

Paper Candy
(702) 256-1745 (fax)
www.papercandy.com

Paper House Productions®
(800) 255-7316
www.paperhouseproductions.
com

Paper Loft
(801) 446-7249
www.paperloft.com

Pebbles Inc.
(801) 224-1857
www.pebblesinc.com

Plaid Enterprises, Inc.
(800) 842-4197
www.plaidonline.com

Polyform Products Co.
(847) 427-0020
www.sculpey.com

Provo Craft® (Wholesale only)
(888) 577-3545
www.provocraft.com

PSX Design™
(800) 782-6748
www.psxdesign.com

Ranger Industries, Inc.
(800) 244-2211
www.rangerink.com

River City Rubber Works
(877) 735-2276
www.rivercityrubberworks.com

Rollabind LLC
(800) 438-3542
www.rollabind.com

Rubba Dub Dub Embellishments
& Art Stamps
(209) 763-2766
www.artsanctum.com

Rusty Pickle
(801) 272-2280
www.rustypickle.com

Sakura of America
(800) 776-6257
www.sakuraofamerica.com

Scrappy Cat Creations™ LLC
(440) 234-4850
www.scrappycatcreations.com

Scrapworks, LLC
(801) 363-1010
www.scrapworks.com

Sizzix
(866) 742-4447
www.sizzix.com

Stampendous!®
(800) 869-0474
www.stampendous.com

Stampin' Up!®
(800) 782-6787
www.stampinup.com

Stampington & Company
(877) STAMPER
www.stampington.com

Sticker Studio
(208) 322-2465
www.stickerstudio.com

Sunday International
(800) 401-8644
www.sundayint.com

Therm O Web, Inc.
(800) 323-0799
www.thermoweb.com

Toybox Rubber Stamps
(707) 431-1400
www.toyboxrubberstamps.com

Tsukineko®, Inc.
(800) 769-6633
www.tsukineko.com

USArtQuest, Inc.
(517) 522-6225
www.usartquest.com

Westrim® Crafts
(800) 727-2727
www.westrimcrafts.com

Wordsworth
(719) 282-3495
www.wordsworthstamps.com

Xyron
(800) 793-3523
www.xyron.com

Index